READING & WRITING
THAI

A WORKBOOK FOR SELF-STUDY

READING & WRITING THAI

A Beginner's Guide to the Thai Alphabet and Pronunciation

by Jintana Rattanakhemakorn

TUTTLE Publishing

Tokyo | Rutland, Vermont | Singapore

Contents

How to Use This Book 6

Part One
The Thai Writing System & Pronunciation
Introduction to the Thai Writing System 8

Part Two
The Lessons
Lesson 1: Consonants 14
Lesson 2: Vowels 32
Lesson 3: Ending Consonants 45
Lesson 4: Tone Marks 47
Lesson 5: Consonant Clusters 57
Lesson 6: Irregular Readings 65
Lesson 7: Reading and Writing Thai Words 72
Lesson 8: Reading Thai Sentences and Short Paragraphs 89
Do-It-Yourself 102
Quizzes 108
Writing a Paragraph 116

Part Three
Appendices
Appendix 1: Thai Basic Phrases 120
Appendix 2: Classifiers 121
Appendix 3: Vegetables 122
Appendix 4: Fruits 124
Appendix 5: Days and Months 125
Appendix 6: Transport 126
Appendix 7: Weight and Length 128

How to Use This Book

Who is this book for?
This book is an easy–to–use guide for beginning-level learners to learn how to read and write Thai without any prior knowledge. It is designed for both self-study and use in a classroom setting. The beginner can begin with the basics and then move on to intermediate lessons within the same book.

What is the purpose of this book?
The primary focus of this book is to provide systematic guidelines which take beginning learners from tracing and copying letters to writing complete words and sentences. Plenty of exercises and writing practice are also included to reinforce the lessons throughout the book.

How is the book structured?
The content will be divided into three main parts:

Part 1: An introduction to the basic Thai writing system and pronunciation guide using Romanizations to help identify and pronounce every Thai consonant and vowel.

Part 2: The main body of the book contains 8 lessons which teach beginners how to write Thai consonants, vowels and tone marks, and will build up to writing and reading words, complete sentences, and short paragraphs. The first three lessons will give you step-by-step guidelines on how to write each character neatly in the correct stroke order, with generous spaces provided for handwriting practice. Each lesson has a set of exercises for reviewing and reinforcing your ability to read, write, and comprehend Thai.

Part 3: A final review gives you additional practice, and at the end of the book audio recordings and printable flashcards will be provided for download. Appendices at the back also allow you to learn some of useful vocabulary and English meanings.

Learning to read and write a new language can be a challenge as you need to go through a fair amount of rote memorization. However, this book contains everything to help you become confident in reading and writing Thai. The lessons will guide you and explain in detail how Thai writing system works. You may find it easier than you expect after all.

Part

1

The Thai Writing System & Pronunciation

Introduction to the Thai Writing System

The earliest Thai writing was found in Sukhothai period, by King Ramkamhaeng in 1283. He devised "The Sukhothai Script" based on the ancient Khmer and Mon scripts, which were derived from southern Indian scripts through the spread of the Buddhist religion and trade contacts in Southeast Asia. Later in the early periods of the Ayutthaya Kingdom, the script called "King Narai script" was reformed and has been used as the national Thai script up to the present.

Thai, like other Indian-based scripts, lists consonants and vowels separately. The Thai script has very complex rules on how letters are pronounced. Often, multiple letters represent the same sound. On the other hand, the sounds of many Thai letters differ depending on whether the letter occurs at the start or the end of a syllable.

In Thai writing, syllables, words, and sentences are written and read from left to right without intervening spaces. Vowels can appear before, above, after, or below a consonant. The consonant always sounds first when pronouncing or reading the syllable. In addition, there is no distinction between uppercase and lowercase letters, and the end of a sentence is marked by a space.

The official language of Thailand, known as Standard Thai, is based on the language spoken in central Thailand. Most people living in central part of Thailand use Standard Thai as their common language, while people in the southern, northern, and northeastern regions are bilingual speakers of Standard Thai and their regional dialects.

Basic Thai grammar

Thai grammar is very easy to understand when comparing with western languages. However, there are some aspects that need to be considered when creating sentences.

Different pronouns are used by male and female speakers. However, subject pronouns and object pronouns are the same (there's no difference between "I" and "me" or "he/she" and "him/her"). The commonly used personal pronouns are:

English Pronoun	Thai Pronoun
I, me (for male speakers)	ผม **phŏm**
I, me (for female speakers)	ฉัน **chăn**
you (polite)	คุณ **khun**
he, she, they	เขา **khăo**
we, us	เรา **rao**

Note: In casual conversation, it's very common that subjects are often omitted, especially "I" and "You". Also, rather than using a personal pronoun, a nickname is often used to refer to yourself or the third person.

- There are no articles like "a", "an", and "the".
- Words are never modified or conjugated for tense, person, possession, singular/plural, gender, or subject-verb agreement.
- Thai sentences follow the same "subject-verb-object" word order as in English.
- No punctuation is used to indicate a question or the end of a Thai sentence.
- In order to form a question, you add a question word at the end of the sentence.

คุณหิวไหม
khun hǐw <u>mái</u>

Are you hungry?

คุณทำอาหารอะไร
khun tham-aa-hǎan <u>à-rai</u>

What are you cooking?

- When talking about quantities of things, you need to add a "classifier," similar to "four sheets of paper" or "three bottles of wine" in English. In Thai however, the number and classifier come after the noun.

noun + number + classifier		
paper + four + sheets	กระดาษ 4 แผ่น **grà-dàat sìi phàehn**	= four sheets of paper
wine + three + bottles	ไวน์ 3 ขวด **waay sǎam khùat**	= three bottles of wine

- Tenses are indicated mostly by using a "timeframe" or helping words at the beginning of or the end of a sentence. In order to state the past and the future in Thai, you can use the following optional words.

  1. Using time words, such as *now*, *today*, *yesterday*, *tomorrow*, *six o'clock*, etc. For example,

     เมื่อวานนี้ฉันไปวัด
     <u>Mûeah-waan-níi</u> chǎn pai wát

     I went to the temple <u>yesterday</u>.

     วันนี้ฉันเหนื่อย
     <u>Wan-níi</u> chǎn nùeay

     I feel tired <u>today</u>.

  2. Using "**láew**" แล้ว (already) at the very end of a sentence to indicate that something was completed before or prior to the moment of speaking. For example,

     ฉันกินยาแล้ว
     Chǎn gin yaa <u>láew</u>

     I've <u>already</u> taken medicine.

     ผมอาบน้ำแล้ว
     Phǒm àap-nám <u>láew</u>.

     I've <u>already</u> taken a bath.

  3. Using "**jà**" จะ (will) in front of verbs to indicate the future, and sometimes you can also include a time word to emphasize when it is going to happen in the future. For example,

     ฉันจะไปตลาด
     chǎn <u>jà</u> pai tà-làat

     I <u>will</u> go to the market.

     เดือนหน้าคุณจะทำอะไร
     Duean-nâa khun <u>jà</u> tham-à-rai?

     What <u>will</u> you do next month?

Pronunciation Guide

Consonants

The following is the basic Thai alphabet. There are 44 letters, which is broken down into 21 initial consonant sounds.

Consonant Form	Consonant Sound	Sounds like	Thai Example
ก	g	as in "get"	กับ gàp
ข ค ฆ	kh	as in "kind"	ขาย khăay
ง	ng	as in "singing"	เงิน ngern
จ	j	as in "joy"	ใจ jai
ฉ ช ฌ	ch	as in "chair"	ชอบ châwp
ซ ศ ษ ส	s	as in "sand"	สอน săwn
ญ ย	y	as in "yes"	ยาย yaay
ฎ ด	d	as in "dog"	ได้ dâi
ฏ ต	t	as in "stand"	ตอน tawn
ฐ ฑ ฒ ถ ท ธ	th	as in "teach"	ทำ tham
ณ น	n	as in "need"	นอน nawn
บ	b	as in "bus"	บ่าย bàay
ป	p	as in "spin"	ปี pii
ผ พ ภ	ph	as in "post"	พี่ phîi
ฝ ฟ	f	as in "fun"	ฟัง fang
ม	m	as in "more"	แม่ mâeh
ร	r	as in "run"	ร้อย róy
ล ฬ	l	as in "long"	เล่น lêhn
ว	w	as in "wet"	วัน wan
ห ฮ	h	as in "have"	ห้า hâa
*อ	*a/e/i/o/u	as in "out"	อ้วน ôuan

*Note: The letter "อ" acts as a silent vowel carrier (a/e/i/o/u) at the beginning of words that start with a vowel.

Ending consonants

There are eight ending sounds. When these consonants appear at the end of a word, they are not voiced aloud.

Form	Sound	Sounds like	Thai Example
ก	k	j	มาก **màak**
ด	t	as in "lou_d_/hi_t_"	ลด **ló_t_**
บ	p	as in "lo_b_/ca_p_"	กลับ **glà_p_**
ง	ng	as in "wro_ng_"	สอง **sǎw_ng_**
น	n	as in "ca_n_"	หวาน **wǎa_n_**
ม	m	as in "di_m_"	ลม **lo_m_**
ย	y	as in "bo_y_"	สวย **sǔa_y_**
ว	w	as in "lo_w_"	ข้าว **khâa_w_**

Vowels

There are 18 single vowels and six further dipthongs, which are generally separated into short and long forms. When speaking of "long" and "short" vowels, this refers to the length of time when the vowel is pronounced. For example, "**naana**" would be an example of a word with a long vowel, where the "a" sound is drawn out to a long duration.

1. Single vowels

Short			Long		
Form		Sound	Form		Sound
_ะ	a	as in "_a_bout"	_า	aa	as in "c_a_r"
◌ิ	i	as in "b_i_n"	◌ี	ii	as in "d_ea_n"
◌ึ	ue	as in "list_en_ (lis_ən_)"	◌ือ	ueh	as in "hmm" (longer)
◌ุ	u	as in "f_oo_t"	◌ู	uu	as in "f_oo_d"
เ_ะ	e	as in "g_e_t" (shorter)	เ_	eh	as in "p_ay_"
แ_ะ	ae	as in "b_a_t" (shorter)	แ_	aeh	as in "d_a_m"
โ_ะ	o	as in "uh-_oh_!" (shorter)	โ_	oh	as in "_owe_"
เ_าะ	aw	as in "h_o_t"	_อ	aw	as in "_or_"
เ_อะ	er	as in "bett_er_" (shorter)	เ_อ	err	as in "p_er_"
			◌ำ	am	as in "g_u_m"
			ไ_ / ใ_	ai	as in "l_ic_"
			เ_า	ao	as in "_ou_t"

2. Diphthongs

Diphthongs are made up of a combination of two single vowels, but the combined sound is pronounced within one syllable.

Short	Long	Sound	
เ◌ียะ	เ◌ีย	(ii + aa) = ia	as in "Liam"
เ◌ือะ	เ◌ือ	(ueh + aa) = uea	no similar sound
◌ัวะ	◌ัว	(uu + aa) = ua	as in "dual"

Tones

Standard Thai has five tones or pitches; *mid, low, falling, high, and rising*. Every Thai word has a particular tone and each tone distinguishes the meaning of one word from another. They are all written with a tone mark except for the neutral mid-level tone, which has no tone mark.

Tone Level	Symbol	Example	Meaning
mid	no mark	คา khaa	to get stuck
low	ˋ	ข่า khàa	Galanga (a plant in the ginger family)
falling	ˆ	ข้า khâa	I, slave, servant
high	ˊ	ค้า kháa	trade
rising	ˇ	ขา khǎa	leg

Part

2

The Lessons

Consonants

The Thai consonant character consists of 44 letters and each one has its own name like in English. For example, the letter "A B C" in English is called '**ei bee cee**'. The following listing follows Thai alphabetical order with the name of each letter. However, two letters in bold type and underline are no longer in use.

ก	ข	<u>ฃ</u>	ค	<u>ฅ</u>
gaw	khǎw	khǎw	khàw	khàw
ฆ	ง	จ	ฉ	ช
khàw	ngàw	jaw	chǎw	chàw
ซ	ฌ	ญ	ฎ	ฏ
sàw	chàw	yàw	daw	taw
ฐ	ฑ	ฒ	ณ	ด
thǎw	thàw	thàw	nàw	daw
ต	ถ	ท	ธ	น
taw	thǎw	thàw	thàw	nàw
บ	ป	ผ	ฝ	พ
baw	paw	phǎw	fǎw	phàw
ฟ	ภ	ม	ย	ร
fàw	phàw	màw	yàw	ràw
ล	ว	ศ	ษ	ส
làw	wàw	sǎw	sǎw	sǎw
ห	ฬ	อ	ฮ	
hǎw	làw	aw	hàw	

Classes of Consonants

These 44 consonants are divided into three groups: Mid, High, and Low. They are classified by their phonetic sounds which can help determine the tone of the syllable.

Mid	High	Low	
ก **gaw**	ข **khǎw**	ค ฆ **khàw**	ง **ngàw**
จ **jaw**	ฉ **chǎw**	ช ฌ **chàw**	ซ **sàw**
ด ฎ **daw**	ถ ฐ **thǎw**	ท ธ ฑ ฒ **thàw**	
ต ฏ **taw**	ผ **phǎw**	พ ภ **phàw**	น ณ **nàw**
บ **baw**	ฝ **fǎw**	ฟ **fàw**	ม **màw**
ป **paw**	ส ศ ษ **sǎw**	ย ญ **yàw**	ร **ràw**
อ **aw**	ห **hǎw**	ล ฬ **làw** / ว **wàw**	ฮ **hàw**

Exercise 1: Trace and write the consonants in Thai alphabetical order.

gaw	
khǎw	
khàw	

khàw

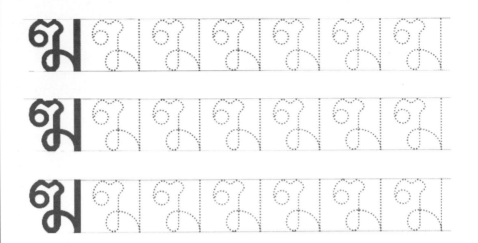

ngàw

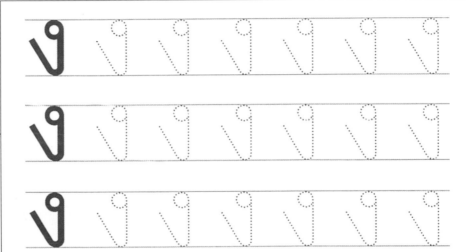

jaw

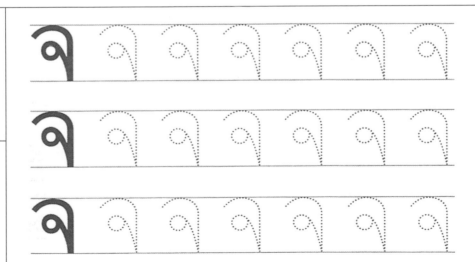

chǎw

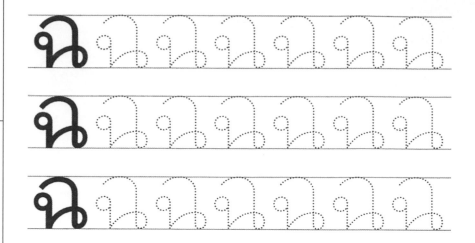

chàw

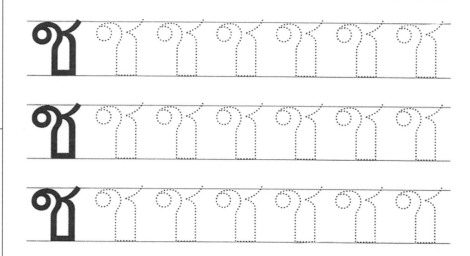

sàw

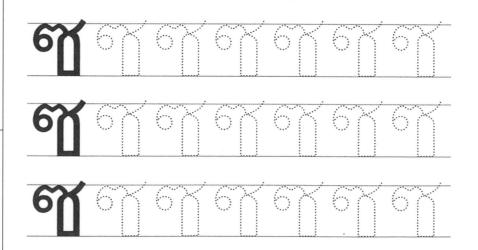

chàw

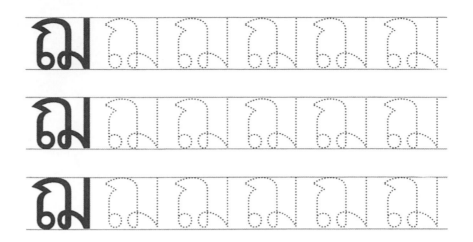

yàw

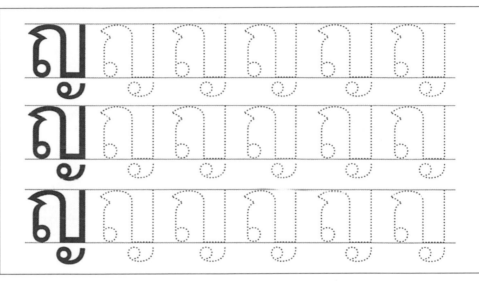

daw

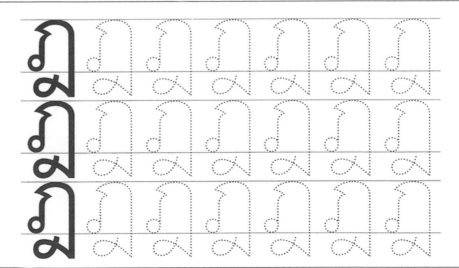

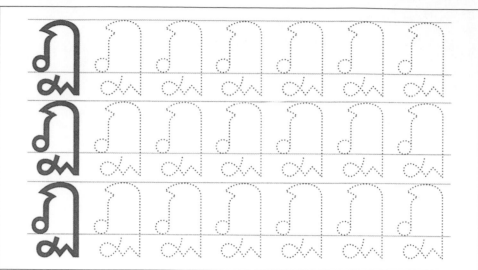

taw

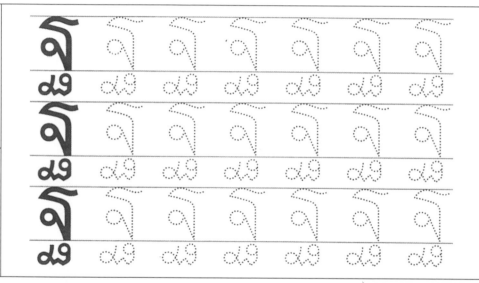

thǎw

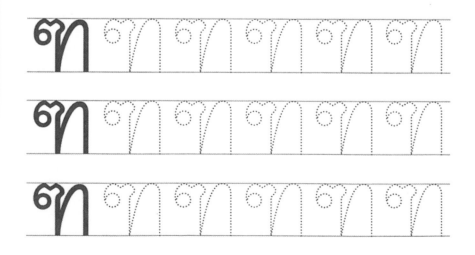

thàw

thàw

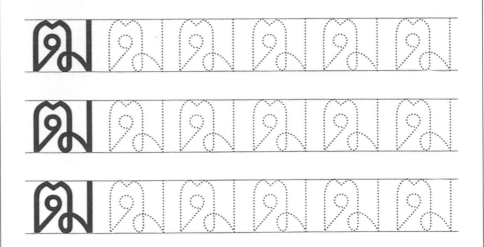

nàw

daw

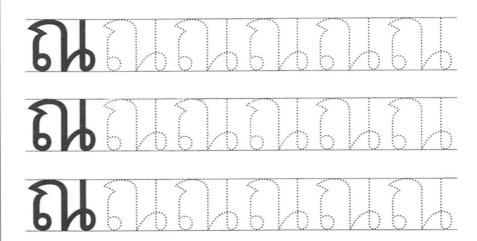

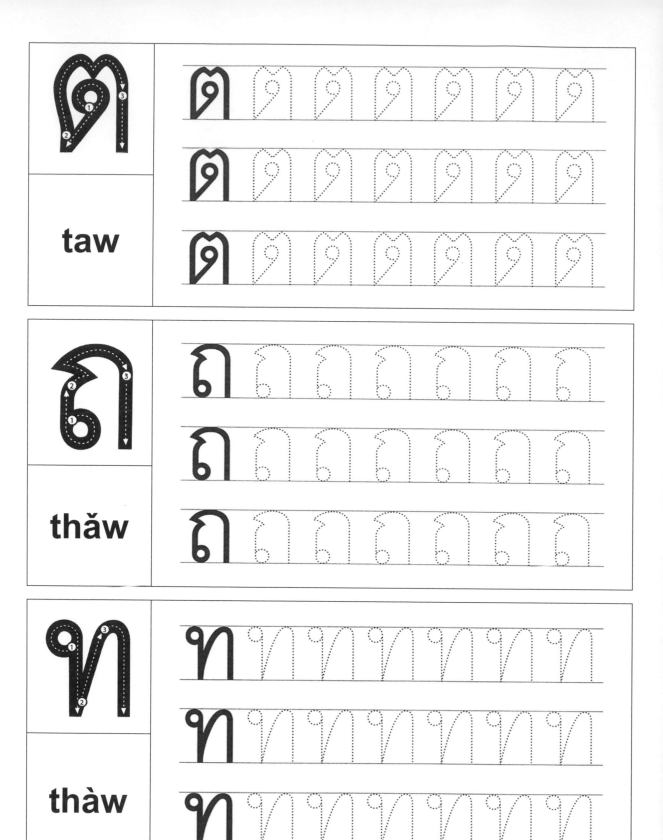

taw

thǎw

thàw

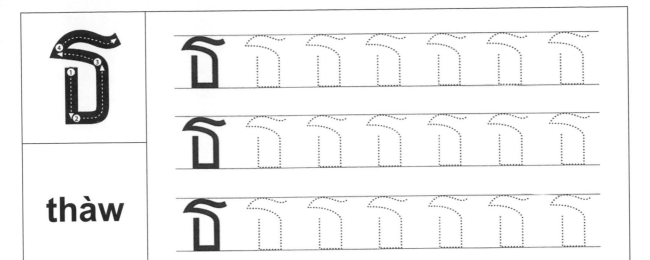

thàw

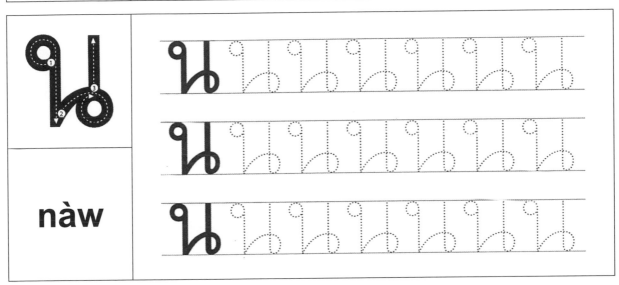

nàw

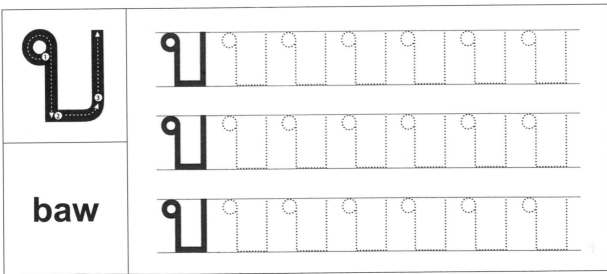

baw

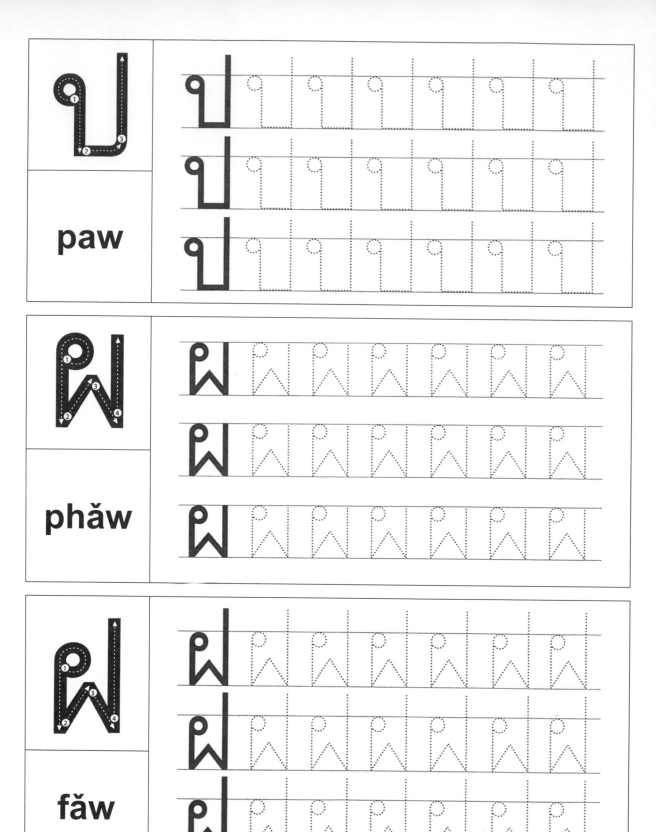

paw

phǎw

fǎw

ผ	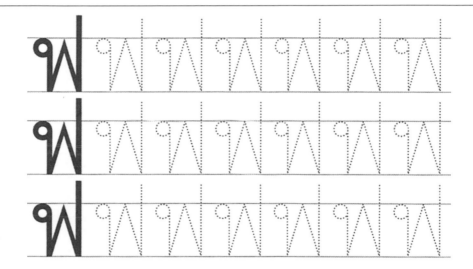
phàw	

ฝ	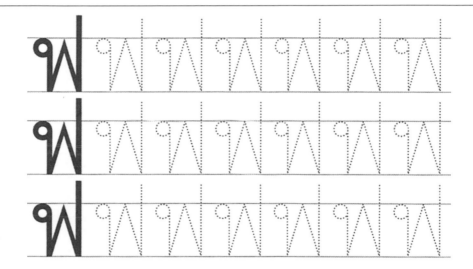
fàw	

	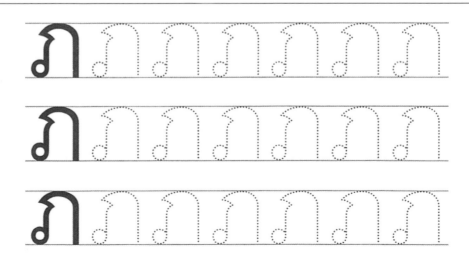
phàw	

màw

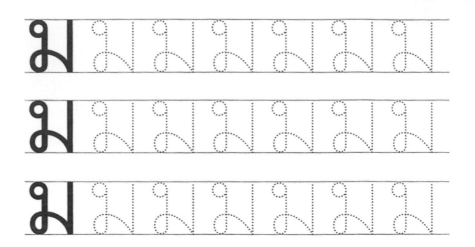

yàw

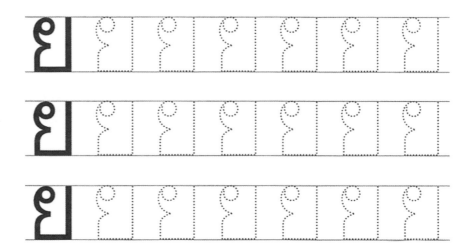

ràw

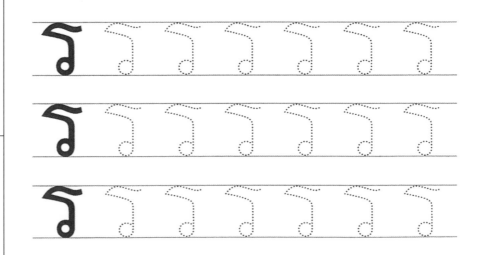

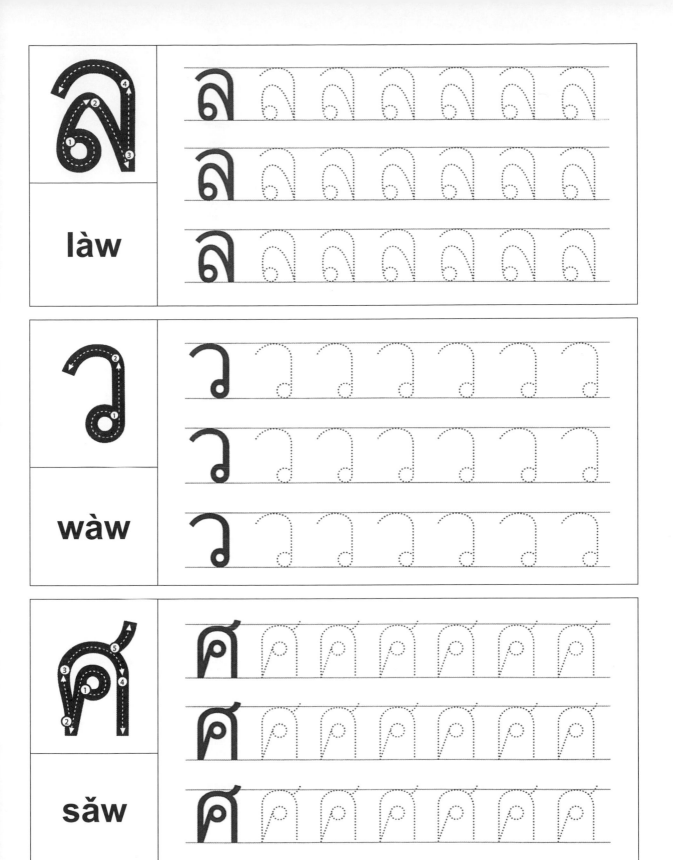

làw

wàw

săw

ยษ **săw**

ส **săw**

ห **hăw**

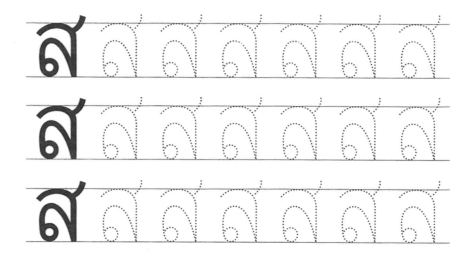

làw

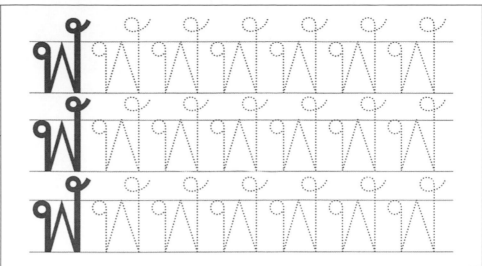

aw

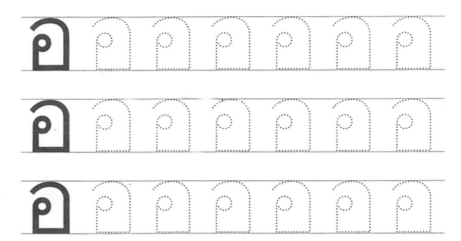

hàw

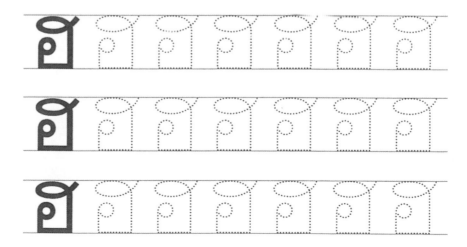

Exercise 2: Identify consonants of each class and write down in the blank below.

ก	บ	ค	ฆ	ง
จ	ฉ	ช	ซ	ฌ
ญ	ฎ	ฏ	ฐ	ฑ
ฒ	ณ	ด	ต	ถ
ท	ธ	น	บ	ป
ผ	ฝ	พ	ฟ	ภ
ม	ย	ร	ล	ว
ศ	ษ	ส	ห	ฬ
อ	ฮ			

1. High consonants

_____

_____

_____

2. Mid consonants

_____

_____

_____

3. Low consonants

_____

_____

_____

🎧 **Exercise 3:** Choose the correct **consonant sound** as you listen to the audio.

1.	ดา	คา	ตา	ถา
2.	ชี	ฉี	ซี	จี
3.	คำ	ดำ	ชำ	ทำ
4.	เค	เด	เต	เฒ
5.	เลา	เสา	เฮา	เฉา
6.	แต	แท	แล	แพ
7.	ไง	ไช	ไซ	ไท
8.	งู	ชู	พู	รู
9.	เจอ	เรอ	เลอ	เวอ
10.	มัว	ตัว	ดัว	วัว
11.	ขอ	ฝอ	สอ	หอ
12.	เกีย	เดีย	เตีย	เบีย
13.	เละ	เทะ	เอะ	เตะ
14.	เรือ	เงือ	เลือ	เจือ
15.	ซอ	ชอ	ขอ	ธอ

Lesson 2 Vowels

There are 28 vowel forms of single vowels and diphthongs, which can go above, below, left of or right of the consonant, or combinations of these positions.

1. Single vowels

Short			Long		
Form	Sound	Example	Form	Sound	Example
_ะ	a	จะ	_า	aa	นา
ิ_	i	ติ	ี_	ii	ปี
ึ_	ue	รึ	ื_อ	ueh	มือ
_ุ	u	ผุ	_ู	uu	หู
เ_ะ	e	เละ	เ_	eh	เข
แ_ะ	ae	แฉะ	แ_	aeh	แพ
โ_ะ	o	โละ	โ_	oh	โผ
เ_าะ	aw	เงาะ	_อ	aw	คอ
เ_อะ	er	เลอะ	เ_อ	err	เธอ
			_ำ	am	ดำ
			ไ_ / ใ_	ai	ไป/ใจ
			เ_า	ao	เสา

2. Diphthongs

Diphthongs are made up of a combination of two single vowels, but they're pronounced within one syllable.

Short			Long		
Form	Sound	Example	Form	Sound	Example
เ_ียะ	ia	เพียะ	เ_ีย	iaa	เสีย
เ_ือะ	uea	เอือะ	เ_ือ	ueah	เรือ
_ัวะ	ua	ยัวะ	_ัว	uaa	หัว

Exercise 1: Trace and write the vowels.

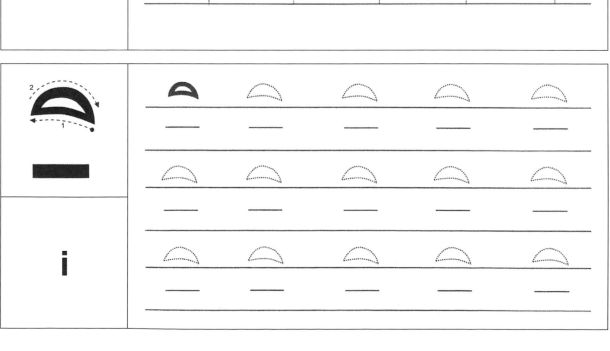

a

aa

i

ii

ue

ueh

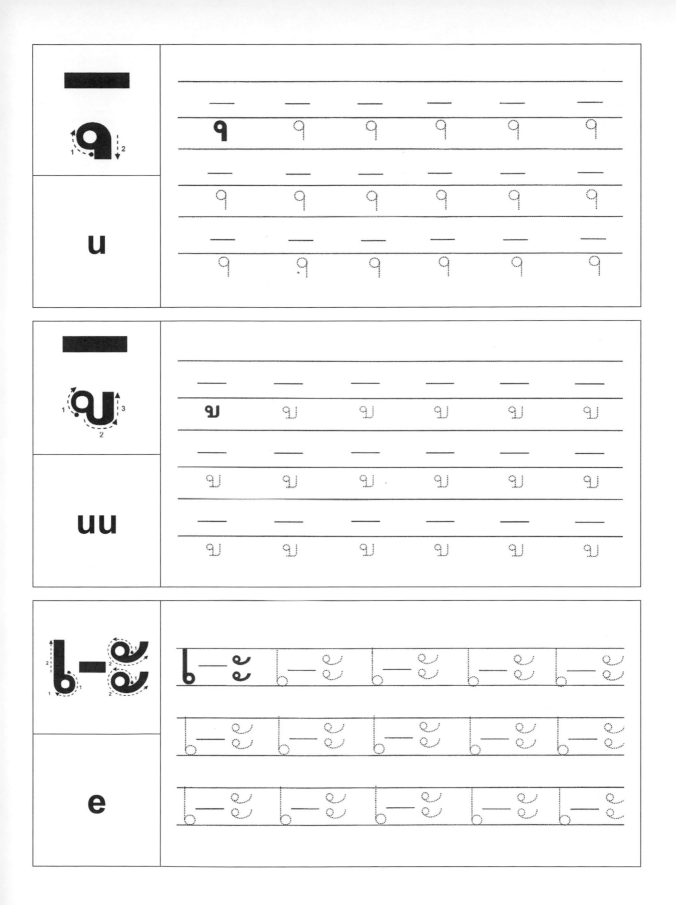

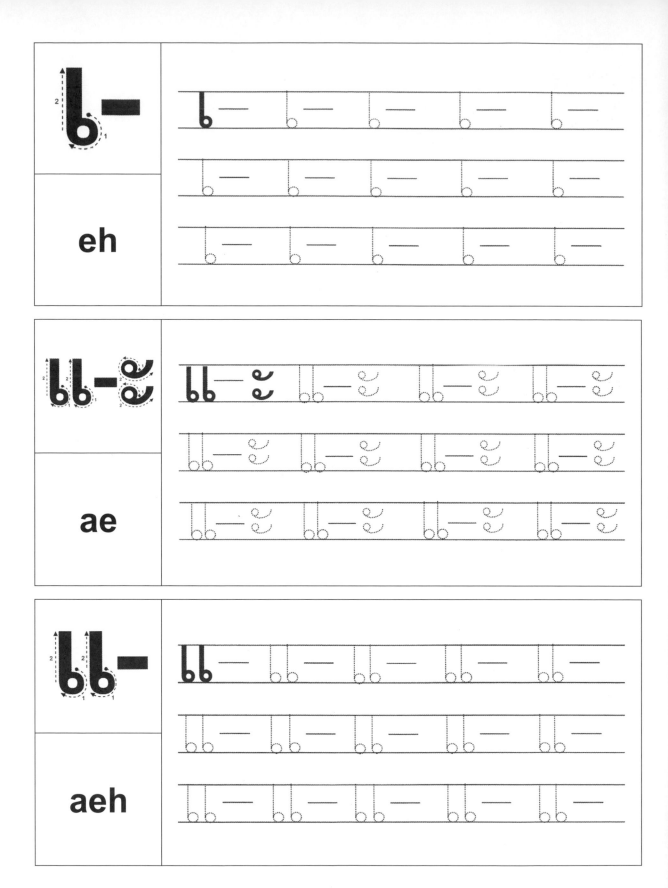

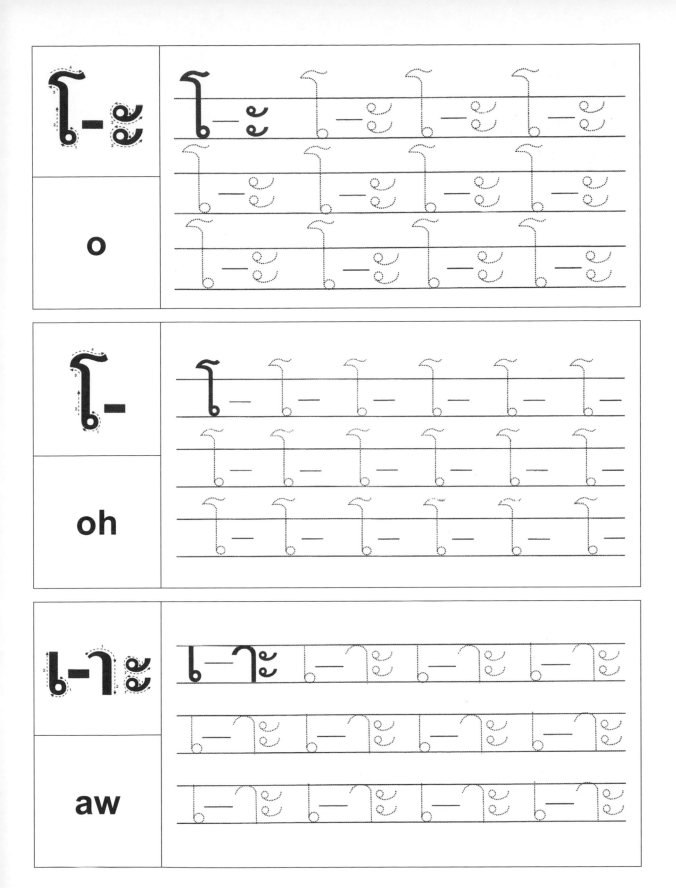

o

oh

aw

aw
(longer)

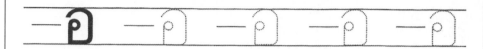

er

err

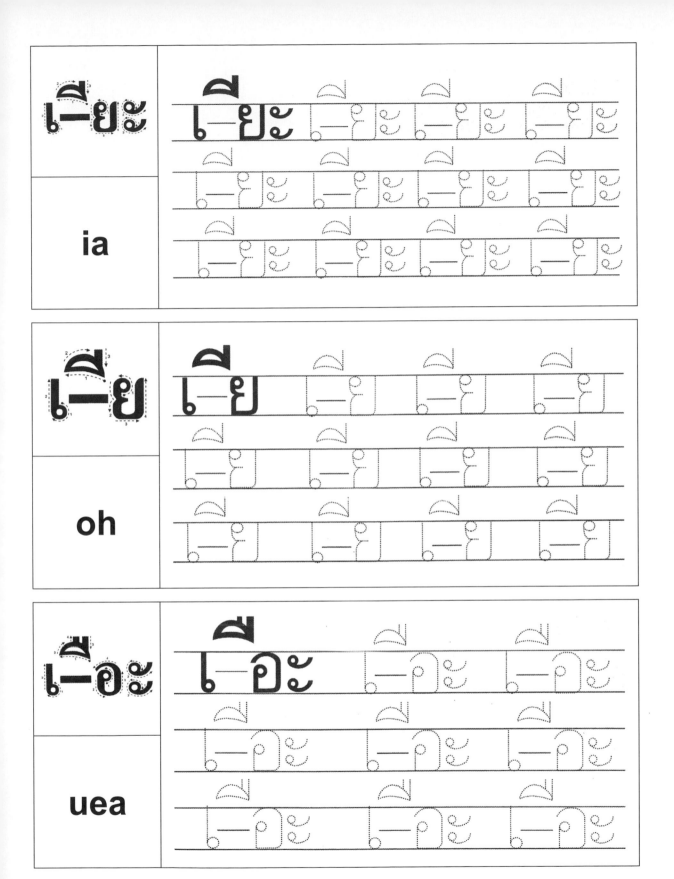

ia

oh

uea

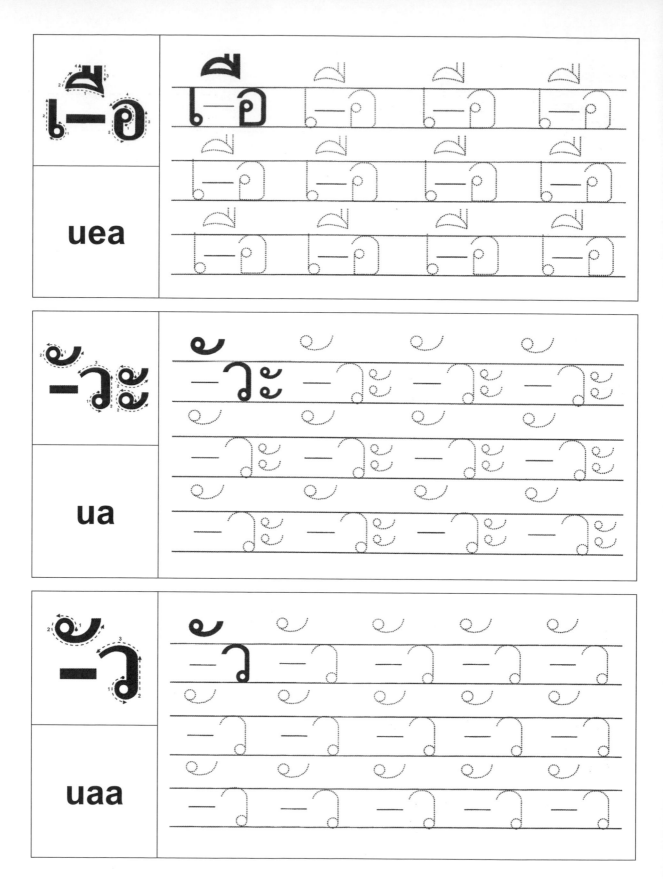

uea

ua

uaa

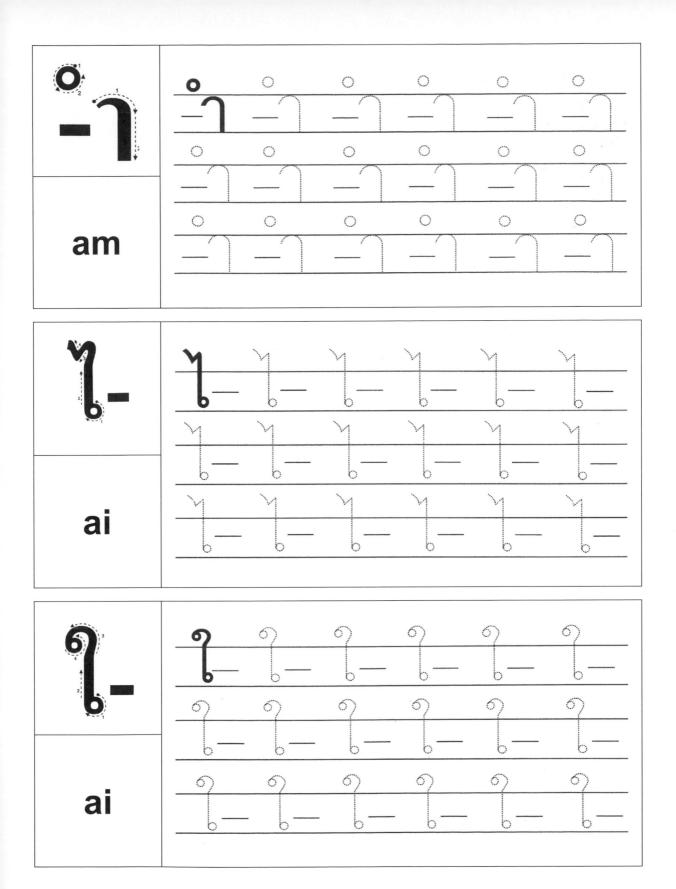

am

ai

ai

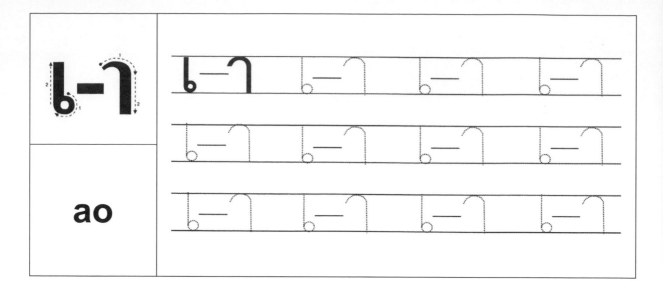

🎧 **Exercise 2:** Choose the correct **vowel sound** as you listen to the audio.

1.	จะ	จุ	เจาะ	จิ
2.	ทา	ที	ไท	เทา
3.	มา	มี	มู	ไม
4.	และ	โละ	ละ	เละ
5.	แพ	พอ	พา	พี
6.	สี	สำ	ไส	เสา
7.	เรือ	ไร	รอ	เรอ
8.	ชุ	ชู	ชิ	ชี
9.	หัว	หอ	หา	เหา
10.	โต	ไต	เตา	ตำ
11.	ยา	ยำ	ไย	เยา
12.	คะ	เคาะ	เคอะ	แคะ
13.	นี	นู	นำ	เนา
14.	เงาะ	เงอะ	งะ	แงะ
15.	บอ	โบ	แบ	เบอ

Vowels Transformation

The following vowels must be changed to new forms when they are followed by the ending consonants.

Vowels	Transformation	New form
-ะ	ฉ + -ะ + น (chǎw + a + nàw)	ฉัน (chǎn)
เ-ะ	ป + เ-ะ + น (paw + e + nàw)	เป็น (pen)
แ-ะ	ท + แ-ะ + ก (thàw + ae + kaw)	แท็ก (tháek)
๎-ว	ส + ๎-ว + น (sǎw + uaa + nàw)	สวน (sǔaan)
เ-อ	ล + เ-อ + ก (làw + err + kaw)	เลิก (lêrrk)
โ-ะ	ผ + โ-ะ + ม (phǎw + o + màw)	ผม (phǒm)

Exercise 3: Rearrange these words.

Vowels Transformation	New form
ฉ + -ะ + น	ฉัน
ข + -ะ + บ	
ส + ๎-ว + ย	
ผ + -ะ + ก	
ล + เ-อ + ก	
ป + เ-ะ + น	

Vowels Transformation	New form
ร + ◌ัว + ย	
ก + -ะ + บ	
ด + เ-อ + น	
ผ + เ-ะ + ด	
ผ + โ-ะ + ม	
น + โ-ะ + ม	
ว + -ะ + ด	
จ + โ-ะ + น	
ผ + -ะ + ด	
ค + เ-ะ + ม	

Lesson 3

Ending Consonants

Many consonants can be used as an ending consonant, but there are only 8 ending consonant sounds, which are divided into 2 types: **stop ending** and **live ending**. A stop-ending sound is formed by completely stopping airflow, while a live ending has a sonorant sound.

✪ Stop ending:

Sound	Form	Examples
-k	-ก -ข -ค -ฆ	จา**ก** (jàak) เล**ข** (lêhk) โช**ค** (chôhk) เม**ฆ** (mêhk)
-t	-ด -ต -ฎ -ฏ -ถ -ฐ -ท -ฒ -ฑ -ธ -จ -ช -ซ -ส -ศ -ษ	เจ็**ด** (jèt) ทั**ต** (thát) กฎ (gòt) ปรากฏ (praa-gòt) นา**ถ** (nâat) รั**ฐ** (rát) บา**ท** (bàat) วุ**ฒิ** (wút) ครุ**ฑ** (khrút) โกร**ธ** (gròht) อา**จ** (àat) รา**ช** (râat) ก๊า**ซ** (gáat) ร**ส** (rót) เก**ศ** (gèht) โท**ษ** (thôht)
-p	-บ -ป -พ -ภ -ฟ	กั**บ** (gàp) บา**ป** (bàap) ภา**พ** (phâap) ลา**ภ** (lâap) ยีรา**ฟ** (yii-láap)

✪ Live ending:

Sound	Form	Examples
-ng	ง	เมือ**ง** (mueang)
-n	-น, -ณ, -ญ, -ร, -ล, -ฬ	กิ**น** (gin) คุ**ณ** (khun) หา**ญ** (hǎan) สา**ร** (sǎan) น้ำตา**ล** (nám-taan) กา**ฬ** (gaan)
-m	ม	ดื่**ม** (dùehm)
-y	ย	ชา**ย** (chaay)
-w	ว	ขา**ว** (khǎaw)

Exercise 1: Write down the Thai consonants that represent each ending consonant sound as listed below.

1. -t	ด,
2. -p	
3. -n	
4. -m	
5. -k	
6. -y	
7. -w	
8. -ng	

Exercise 2: Write down the ending consonant sound of each word. The first box has been done as an example.

word	ending sound	word	ending sound
ขาย	y	ผม	
อัญ		แข็ง	
สุข		วัด	
กฎ		เดียว	
ภาพ		ทิศ	

Exercise 3: Find a pair of word that has the <u>**same ending consonant sound**</u>. The first one has been done as an example.

ขาน	เลข	บาป	รัฐ	เอก	เพียร	กาจ	ภาพ	ชาญ	วาฬ

ขาน	ชาญ

4 Tone Marks

Tones are an integral part of words in Thai. Using the wrong tone can change the meaning of a word. In written Thai, the tone mark is used to indicate the tone of a word or syllable. However, tone marks do not always represent the same tone.

Thai has five distinctive tones; *mid, low, falling, high, and rising.* They all carry tone marks except for the mid tone. Whether there is no tone mark, the tone is always there.

Tone Marks	Tone Level	Symbol
No mark	mid	No symbol
ı	low	`
ฆ	falling	^
ฒ	high	´
✚	rising	ˇ

Exercise 1: Trace and write the tone marks.

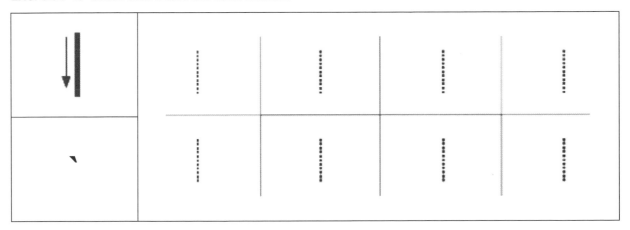

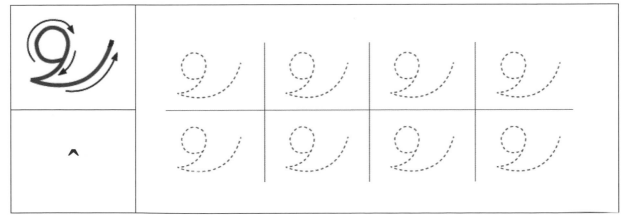

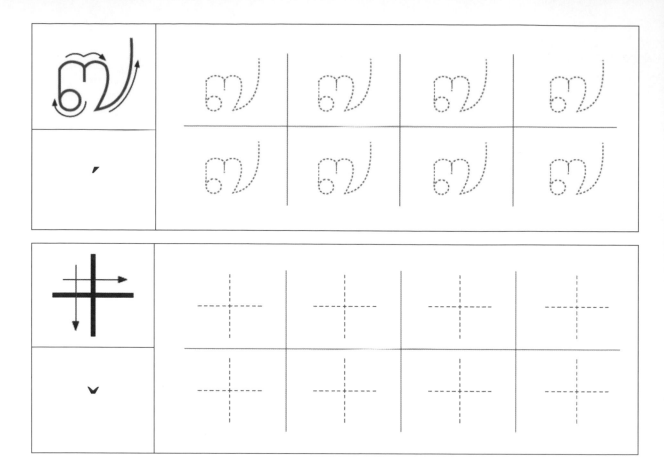

Tone Marks Position

Tone marks are always placed above the initial consonant of the syllable.

Examples: ไม่   ร้าน   เป้า

If the consonant has a superscript vowel, the tone mark is placed above that vowel.

Examples: ซื้อ   กี่   เพื่อน

In case of a double consonant, the tone mark is placed above the second consonant.

Examples: อร่อย   หน้า   สร้าง

Tone rules

Tones are an essential part of Thai words. Using the wrong tone can change the meaning of a word. In order to know how to make accurate tones and know how different they sound, it is important to learn about the tonal composition of Thai syllables and the tone rules.

The tone of a syllable is determined by a combination of the following factors:

1. Class of initial consonant: high, mid, or low
2. Type of vowel: short vowel or long vowel
3. Type of ending consonant: stop ending or live ending
4. Tone mark (if any)

Summary of the tone rules:

I. Mid consonants + vowels + tone marks

Mid Consonants	Long vowels	Short vowels	Tone marks			
			᠄	**◡**	**๗**	**✛**
ก จ ด ต บ ป ฎ ฏ	→ กา **gaa**		↓ ก่า **gàa**	⌢ ก้า **gâa**	↗ ก๊า **gáa**	◡ ก๋า **găa**
		↓ กะ **gà**			↗ ก๊ะ **gá**	

🎧 Reading Practice

Vowel	No mark →	᠄ ↓	◡ ⌢	๗ ↗	✛ ◡
-า	กา **gaa**	ก่า **gàa**	ก้า **gâa**	ก๊า **gáa**	ก๋า **găa**
◌ี	ปี **pii**	ปี่ **pìi**	ปี้ **pîi**	ปี๊ **píi**	ปี๋ **pĭi**
◌ือ	ตือ **tueh**	ตื่อ **tùeh**	ตื้อ **tûeh**	ตื๊อ **túeh**	ตื๋อ **tŭeh**
◌ู	ดู **duu**	ดู่ **dùu**	ดู้ **dûu**	ดู๊ **dúu**	ดู๋ **dŭu**
-ะ		กะ **gà**		ก๊ะ **gá**	
◌ิ		จิ **jì**		จิ๊ **jí**	
◌ึ		อึ **uè**		อึ๊ **ué**	
◌ุ		บุ **bù**		บุ๊ **bú**	

2. High consonants + vowels + endings + tone marks

High Consonants	Long Vowels	Short Vowels	Tone marks			
			I	๏	๛	+
	◡	↓	↓	◠		
ข ฉ ถ ฐ ผ ฝ ส ศ ษ ห	ขา **khǎa**	เขะ **khè**	ข่า **khàa**	ข้า **khâa**		

🎧 Reading Practice

Long Vowels	No mark	I	๏	๛	+
	◡	↓	◠		
เ-	เข **khěh**	เข่ **khèh**	เข้ **khêh**		
แ-	แฉ **chǎeh**	แฉ่ **chàeh**	แฉ้ **châeh**		
โ-	โถ **thǒh**	โถ่ **thòh**	โถ้ **thôh**		
-อ	หอ **hǎw**	ห่อ **hàw**	ห้อ **hâw**		
เ-อ	เฝอ **fěrr**	เฝ่อ **fèrr**	เฝ้อ **fêrr**		

Short Vowels	No mark	่	้	๊	๋
	↓				
เ-ะ	เสะ **sè**				
แ-ะ	แฉะ **chàe**				
โ-ะ	โผะ **phò**				
เ-าะ	เถาะ **thàw**				
เ-อะ	เหอะ **hèr**				

3. Low consonants + vowels + tone marks

Low Consonants	Long Vowels	Short Vowels	Tone marks			
			่	้	๊	๋
คงชฌฑ ธ ฒฆรนณม วยญลฬ	→ มา **măa**		⤾ ม่า **mâa**	↗ ม้า **máa**		
		↗ มะ **má**	⤾ ม่ะ **mâ**			

🎧 Reading Practice

Long Vowels	No mark	่	้	๊	๋
	→	⌒	↗		
◌ู	คู khuu	คู่ khûu	คู้ khúu		
โ◌	โง ngoh	โง่ ngôh	โง้ ngóh		
◌ือ	ชือ chueh	ชื่อ chûeh	ชื้อ chúeh		
◌า	นา naa	น่า nâa	น้า náa		
เ◌	เท theh	เท่ thêh	เท้ théh		
◌อ	พอ ngoh	พ่อ ngoh	พ้อ ngoh		
แ◌	แว waeh	แว่ wâeh	แว้ wáeh		
◌ู	รู ruu	รู่ rûu	รู้ rú		
◌ี	ยี yii	ยี่ yîi	ยี้ yíi		

Short Vowels	No mark	่	้	๊	๋
		⌒	↗		
◌ะ		ค่ะ khâ	คะ khá		
เ◌อะ		เน่อะ nêr	เนอะ nér		

4. Mid consonants + vowels + endings + tone marks

Mid Consonants	Long vowels	Short vowels	Tone marks			
			่	้	๊	๋
live ending	→ กาน gaan	→ กัน gan	↓ ก่าน gàan	⌒ ก้าน gâan	↗ ก๊าน gáan	⌣ ก๋าน gǎan
stop ending	↓ กาก gàak	↓ กัด gàt			↗ ก๊าก gáak	

5. High consonants + vowels + endings + tone marks

High Consonants	Long vowels	Short vowels	Tone marks			
			่	้	๊	๋
live ending	⌣ ขาย khǎay	⌣ ขัย khay	↓ ข่าย khàay	⌒ ข้าย khâay		
stop ending	↓ ขาด khàat	↓ ขัด khàt				

6. Low consonants + vowels + endings + tone marks

Low Consonants	Long vowels	Short vowels	Tone marks			
			่	้	๊	๋
live ending	→ แมน maehn	→ มัน man	⌒ แม่น mâehn	↗ แม้น máehn		
stop ending	⌒ มาก mâak			↗ ม้าก máak		
		↗ มัด mát				

Exercise 1: Identify the tone of the following words.

Word	Tone				
น้ำ	→	↓	⌢	↗	⌣
โต๊ะ	→	↓	⌢	↗	⌣
เก่า	→	↓	⌢	↗	⌣
ได้	→	↓	⌢	↗	⌣
เป๊ะ	→	↓	⌢	↗	⌣
พี่	→	↓	⌢	↗	⌣
แฉะ	→	↓	⌢	↗	⌣
หัว	→	↓	⌢	↗	⌣
เสือ	→	↓	⌢	↗	⌣
เจาะ	→	↓	⌢	↗	⌣
อุ๊	→	↓	⌢	↗	⌣
พ่อ	→	↓	⌢	↗	⌣

Exercise 2: Underline the right tone as you listen to the audio.

1. ใส   ใส่   ใส้

2. บาง   บ่าง   บ้าง

3. ยัว   ยั่ว   ยั้ว

4. เชือ   เชื่อ   เชื้อ

5. ดวน   ด่วน   ด้วน

6. ผู   ผู่   ผู้

7. นอน   น่อน   น้อน

8. เพียง   เพี่ยง   เพี้ยง

9. หิว   หิ่ว   หิ้ว

10. เริม   เริ่ม   เริ้ม

Exercise 3: Split the components of each word.

Word	Consonant	Long vowel	Short vowel	Live ending	Stop ending	Tone mark	Tone
แก้ม	ก	แ-	-	ม	-	๋	◠
น้อง							
เชื่อม							
เสียบ							
กั๊ก							
คาบ							
ซึ้ง							
ฉวย							

Word	Consonant	Long vowel	Short vowel	Live ending	Stop ending	Tone mark	Tone
เห็น							
โรค							
ทิศ							
ภาพ							
ต้ม							
ถอด							
เดี๋ยว							
บ๊วย							
ลื่น							
ธูป							

Lesson  Consonant Clusters

Clusters are made of two consonant sounds that appear together with no vowels at the beginning of a syllable as initial consonants. Consonant clusters can be divided into 3 types:
1. Real cluster
2. Unreal cluster
3. Leading consonants cluster

1. Real cluster:

It is a combination of two consonants in which the first consonant is blended with ร /r/, ล /l/, ว /w/. When reading out, they are pronounced together. There are 15 forms but 11 sounds.

First Consonant	Second Consonant					
	ร /r/		ล /l/		ว /w/	
ก	กร gr	กราบ gràap	กล gl	ไกล glai	กว gw	กวาง gwaang
ข	ขร khr	ขรุขระ khrù-khrà	ขล khl	ขลุ่ย khlùy	ขว khw	ขวาน khwǎan
ค	คร khr	ครู khruu	คล khl	คลอง khlawng	คว khw	ควาย khwaay
ต	ตร tr	ตรา traa	-	-	-	-
ป	ปร pr	ปรับ pràp	ปล pl	เปล่า plào	-	-
พ	พร phr	พริก phrík	พล phl	เพลีย phlia	-	-
ผ	-	-	ผล phl	ผลิ phlì	-	-

Note: The tone mark is placed over the second consonant; however the tone is determined by the class of the first consonant.

Examples	Reading
ขว้าง	khwâang
คล่อง	khlâwng
ปลื้ม	plûehm
ใกล้	glâi
พรุ่ง	phrûng

📖 **Practice reading the following words**

กว่า **gwàa**	เคลือบ **khlûeahp**	ขวา **khwǎa**	ครัว **khrua**	ไตร **trai**
เปล่า **plào**	กลับ **glàp**	เผลอ **phlěrr**	เปรี้ยว **phrîaw**	ความ **khwaam**
เกลือ **glueah**	คล้าย **khláay**	พร้อม **phráwm**	เพลง **phlehng**	กรอง **grawng**

Exercise 1: Split the components of each word

Word	Consonant	Vowel	Ending	Tone mark	Tone
กรอบ	กร	-อ	บ	-	↓
ขว้าง					
โคร่ง					
เปรอะ					
กล้วย					
พร่ำ					

Word	Consonant	Vowel	Ending	Tone mark	Tone
ขลุ่ย					
แคว้น					
เปรี้ยว					
เคร่ง					
ตรง					

2. Unreal cluster

A cluster is pronounced as a single sound, even though two consonants are positioned together.

a. When "ร" appears with one of these four initial consonants (จ, ซ, ศ, ส), it is silent.

Consonant cluster	Word	Reading
จร	จริง	จิง **jing**
ซร	ไซร้	ไซ้ **sái**
ศร	เศร้า	เส้า **sâo**
สร	สร้าง	ส้าง **sâang**

b. The cluster form is /ทร/ but it is pronounced as /ซ/.

Consonant cluster	Word	Reading
ทร	ทราบ	ซาบ **sâap**
	แทรก	แซก **sâehk**
	ทรุด	ซุด **sút**
	โทรม	โซม **sohm**
	ไทร	ไซ **sai**

Exercise 2: Write the following words in Thai pronunciation and romanization. The first word has been done as an example.

Word	Reading	
จริง	จิง	jing
เสริม		
สระ		
เสร็จ		
ศรี		
ทราย		
ทรวง		
ทรง		
ศรัทธา		
อินทรี		

3. Leading consonant cluster

a. Leading "ห"

When the letter "ห" precedes the following low consonants: ง, ญ, น, ม, ย, ร, ล, ว, it is unpronounced. However, this initial high consonant leads these low consonants into the high consonant tone rules.

Consonants	Long vowel	Short vowel	Tone marks			
			่	้	๊	๋
(ห) ง ญ น ม ย ร ล ว	꜖ หนา		↓ หน่า	꜔ หน้า		
		↓ หนะ				

📖 **Practice reading the following words.**

หง-	หญ-	หน-	หม-	หย-	หร-	หล-	หว-
หงาย **ngǎay**	หญิง **yǐng**	หนัง **nǎng**	หมอ **mǎw**	หยอก **yàwk**	หรือ **rǔeh**	หลา **lǎa**	หวาย **wǎay**
หงอน **ngǎwn**	ใหญ่ **yài**	หนอน **nǎwn**	หมา **mǎa**	หยาม **yǎam**	เหรอ **rěrr**	หลอก **làwk**	แหวน **wǎehn**
เหงา **ngǎo**	หญ้า **yâa**	หนู **nǔu**	หมี **mǐi**	เหยิน **yěrrn**	หรอก **ràwk**	เหลา **lǎo**	หวาน **wǎan**
หงา **ngǎa**	-	หนาม **nǎam**	ไหม **mǎi**	หยี **yǐi**	หรู **rǔu**	เหลือง **lǔeahng**	หวอ **wǎw**
หงำ **ngǎm**	-	หนำ **nǎm**	เหมือน **mǔeahn**	แหยม **yǎehm**	หรา **rǎa**	หลาย **lǎay**	หวุด **wùt**
เหงือก **ngǔeahk**	-	เหนือ **nǔeah**	หมู **mǔu**	หย่อม **yàwm**	หรี่ **rìi**	แหลม **lǎehm**	หวิด **wìt**

b. Leading "อ"

Mid consonant "อ" is paired with low consonant "ย". In this case, "อ" is silent but it leads "ย" into the mid consonant tone rules. There are **only four words** with "อย-" spelling.

Form	Word	Reading
อย	อย่า	**yàa**
	อยู่	**yùu**
	อย่าง	**yàang**
	อยาก	**yàak**

🎧 **Exercise 3:** Identify the tones of the following words:

หมา ⌣	ใหญ่ ___	หลับ ___	หมู่ ___
หรือ ___	หยาม ___	หวาน ___	อย่า ___
หนัก ___	หวัด ___	เหงือก ___	หมุน ___
แหวน ___	อย่าง ___	หมอก ___	อยู่ ___
อยาก ___	โหล ___	เหงา ___	เหยื่อ ___

c. Non-conforming cluster

It is a combination of two consonants, which their sounds are apart. The first consonant must be pronounced with an unwritten short vowel "-ะ" in conformance with the tone of its own consonant class, while the second one acts as the initial consonant of the next syllable. There are two types of this cluster.

(1) Mid consonant + Low consonant

When a mid consonant leads a low consonant, the initial is pronounced with a short vowel "-ะ" while the latter is pronounced according to the rules for high consonants.

Form	Word	Reading	
กน-	กนก	กะ-หนก	gà-nòk
ตล-	ตลาด	ตะ-หลาด	tà-làat
อร-	อร่อย	อะ-หร่อย	à-ràwy
จร-	จรวด	จะ-หรวด	jà-rùat

(2) High consonant + Low consonant

In the case of a high consonant leading a low consonant, the first syllable is pronounced with a short vowel "-ะ" while the second one is pronounced according to the rules for high consonants.

Form	Word	Reading	
ขน-	ขนม	ขะ-หนม	khà-nǒm
ฉล-	ฉลอง	ฉะ-หลอง	chà-lǎwng
ผล-	ผลึก	ผะ-หลึก	phà-lùek
ถน-	ถนน	ถะ-หนน	thà-nǒn

Note: There are some "non-conforming" clusters in which each consonant governs the tone of its own syllable in accordance with the rules of its own consonant class. Here are some examples.

- High consonant leading mid consonant

Word	Reading	
สบาย	สะ-บาย	**sà-baay**
แสดง	สะ-แดง	**sà-daehng**

- Low consonant leading low consonant

Word	Reading	
ทนาย	ทะ-นาย	**thá-naay**
ชนิด	ชะ-นิด	**chá-nít**

- High consonant leading high consonant

Word	Reading	
สหาย	สะ-หาย	**sà-hǎay**
ผสม	ผะ-สม	**phà-sǒm**

Exercise 4: Write the following words in Thai pronunciation and romanization. The first word has been done as an example.

(1) Mid consonant + Low consonant

Word	Reading	
อร่อย	อะ-หร่อย	**à-ràwy**
จมูก		
จรวด		
ตลาด		
ตลก		

Word	Reading	
อนึ่ง		
อร่าม		
จริต		
องุ่น		

(2) High consonant + Low consonant

Word	Reading	
ขนม	ขะ-หนม	khà-nǒm
ผนัง		
ขยัน		
ฉลาด		
ถนอม		
ฝรั่ง		
สนาม		
สนุก		
ฉลอง		

Lesson **6** Irregular Readings

There are some unusual written forms in Thai that do not follow the pronunciation rules.

1. Double consonant "-รร"

a. When an initial is combined with "-รร" without an ending consonant, it is pronounced as "-ัน" [-**an**].

Word	Reading	
สรร	สัน	sǎn
บรรทัด	บัน-ทัด	ban-thát
พรรษา	พัน-สา	phan-sǎa

b. If an initial is combined with "-รร" and has an ending consonant, it is pronounced as "-ั + ending."

Word	Reading	
กรรม	กัม	gam
พรรค	พัก	phák
ธรรม	ทัม	tham
วรรณ	วัน	wan

2. Ending consonant "-ร"

If "-ร" is at the end of a word, it can be pronounced as "-อ + น = -อน."

Word	Reading	
กร	กอน	gawn
พร	พอน	phawn
อาทร	อา-ทอน	aa-thawn
ลูกศร	ลูก-สอน	lûuk-sǎwn

3. Medial consonant

There may be one consonant situated in the middle of a word which has a double function:
1. It acts as the ending of the first syllable and is pronounced according to the rules given for an ending consonant.
2. It performs as the initial of the next syllable and is pronounced with an unwritten short vowel "-ะ" in conformance with the tone of its own consonant class.

Word	Reading	
ผลไม้	<u>ผน-ละ-ไม้</u>	phǒn-lá-mái
ศาสนา	<u>สาด-สะ-หนา</u>	sàat-sà-nǎa
รัฐบาล	<u>รัด-ถะ-บาน</u>	rát-thà-baan
พัฒนา	<u>พัด-ทะ-นา</u>	phát-thá-naa

4. Extra ending consonants

a. There are two forms of ending: "-ติ" and "-ตุ", which can be used as "ด" /t/.

Word	Reading	
ชาติ	ชาด	châat
เหตุ	เหด	hèht

b. In some words, double consonants "-รถ" and "-ตร" at the end of the word can be used as "ด" /t/.

Spelling	Reading	
สามารถ	สา-มาด	sǎa-mâat
ตักบาตร	ตัก-บาด	tàk-bàat

5. Special characters from Sanskrit: ฤ ฤๅ

a. "ฤ" can be pronounced in three different ways: รึ (rúe), ริ (rí), เรอ (rer), depending on its position in a word.
  • If "ฤ" appears as an initial consonant, it's pronounced as รึ (rúe).

Spelling	Reading	
ฤดู	รึ-ดู	rúe-duu
ฤดี	รึ-ดี	rúe-dee

- If "ฤ" follows the following consonants: **ค น พ ม ห**, it's also pronounced as รี (**rúe**).

Word	Reading	
นฤเบศ	นะ-รึ-เบด	ná-rúe-bèht
พฤติกรรม	พรึด-ติ-กัม	phrúet-tì-gam
หฤโหด	หะ-รึ-โหด	hà-rúe-hòht

- If "ฤ" appears as an initial consonant with an ending consonant, it's pronounced as ริ (**rí**).

Word	Reading	
ฤทธิ์	ริด	rít
ฤทธา	ริด-ทา	rít-thaa

- If "ฤ" follows the following consonants: **ก ต ท ป ศ ส**, it's pronounced as ริ (**rí**).

Word	Reading	
ตฤณ	ตริน	trin
ทฤษฎี	ทริด-สะ-ดี	thrít-sà-dii

- If "ฤ" precedes "ก," it's pronounced as เรอ (**rer**). But there is only word.

Word	Reading	
ฤกษ์	เริก	rêrrk

b. "ฤๅ" can be pronounced as รือ (**rueh**).

Word	Reading	
ฤๅษี	รือ-สี	rueh-sĭi

6. Special reading with "–อ" vowel

In some cases, when an initial consonant without any vowel precedes "ริ," it is pronounced as combining with the -อ (-**aw**) vowel.

Word	Reading	
บริษัท	บอ-ริ-สัด	baw-rí-sàt
บริการ	บอ-ริ-กาน	baw-rí-gaan
มรณา	มอ-ระ-นา	maw-rá-naa
ธรณี	ทอ-ระ-นี	thaw-rá-nii

Exercise 1: Write the correct reading form of the following words. The first one has been completed as an example.

Word	Reading	
สร้างสรรค์	ส้าง-สัน	sâang-săn
เหตุผล		
ปฏิบัติ		
บรรยาย		
ธรรมชาติ		
ฆาตกร		
พฤกษา		
ธุรกิจ		
สามารถ		
บริโภค		
ผลไม้		
พฤหัส		

Word	Reading	
ทรหด		
ฤทัย		
ราชวัง		
ถาวร		

7. Special symbols

a. Sound killer (ฺ) or **การันต์ (gaa-ran)**

This symbol (ฺ) is called **การันต์ (gaa-ran)** and used to indicate a silent letter by placing it on top of the excess ending consonant. Most words with **การันต์ (gaa-ran)** are borrowed words from western and eastern languages, e.g. English, Pali, and Sanskrit.

Word	Reading	
ศุกร์	สุก	**sùk**
ศูนย์	สูน	**sǔnn**
แพทย์	แพด	**phâeht**
จอห์น (John)	จอน	**jawn**
เบียร์ (beer)	เบีย	**bia**
แอร์ (air)	แอ	**aeh**
ทัวร์ (tour)	ทัว	**thua**

b. Reduplication symbol "ๆ" or **ไม้ยมก (mái yá-mók)**

Instead of writing the same word twice, "ๆ" or **ไม้ยมก (mái yá-mók)** is placed after a word to indicate repetition. It is often used to emphasize or intensify the meaning. When writing, there should be a space before and after "ๆ".

Word	Reading	
มากๆ	มาก มาก	**mâak mâak**
เด็กๆ	เด็ก เด็ก	**dèk dèk**

c. Abbreviation marker "ฯ" or ไปยาลน้อย (**pai-yaan-nóy**)

It is used to shorten words or phrases and placed after the shortened ones, without any space between them.

Full form	Short form	Reading
กรุงเทพมหานคร	กรุงเทพฯ	**grung-thêhp**
วัดพระเชตุพนวิมลมังคลาราม	วัดพระเชตุพนฯ	**wát phrá-cheh-tù-phon**

d. Etcetera "ฯลฯ" or ไปยาลใหญ่ (**pai-yaan-yài**)

It is a punctuation mark like *etc.* in English and placed at the end of a list without a comma. For example, in the following expression:

ของที่ขายในตลาดมี เนื้อสัตว์ ผัก ผลไม้ น้ำตาล น้ำปลา ฯลฯ

khǎwng thîi khǎay nai tà-làat mii núeh-sàt phàk phŏn-lá-mái náam-taan náam-plaa ฯลฯ

(There are many things being sold in the market, such as meats, vegetables, fruits, sugar, fish sauce, etc.)

🎧 **Exercise 2:** Choose the right word as you listen to the audio.

ไกล	ใกล้	กลาย
ฉลาด	ตลาด	ฉลาก
หมอ	หมา	หมอน
ปราย	ปลาย	ปลา
อยาก	อย่าง	อย่า
เพื่อน	เพิ่ม	เพิ่ง
ช่วย	เชื่อ	ชั่ว
แหวน	หวาน	หวาย
สวย	สวน	สวม
วัน	วาน	หวัน
บริขาร	บริวาร	บริการ

ฤษี	ฤดี	ฤดู
ไทร	ทราย	ไซร้
ขยาย	ขยาน	ขยัน
ง่วง	ง่วน	งั่ว
คลอง	คล่อง	คล้อง
ผล	พล	พร
ไย	ยาย	ใหญ่
โทด	ทอด	ถอด
จอน	โจน	จน

Reading and Writing Thai Words

Unlike English and other languages, Thai is traditionally written from left to right without using punctuation or spaces between words in a sentence. However, spacing is only used in the following conditions:

- making a list of words or phrases, i.e. ฉันชอบกินผลไม้ เช่น กล้วย มะม่วง ส้ม และ ฝรั่ง (**chăn châwp gin phŏn-lá-mái chêhn glûay má-mûang sôm láeh fà-ràng**)
- finishing a phrase, clause or sentence and starting a new one again, i.e. ฉันเป็นนักศึกษา ฉันเรียนที่มหาวิทยาลัยขอนแก่น (**chăn pen nák-sùek-săa chăn rian thîi má-hăa-wít-thá-yaa-lai**)

Thai syllable structure is composed of four parts: initial consonant (C), vowel (V), ending (E), and tone mark (T).

> Initial consonant + Vowel + Ending (optional) + Tone mark (optional)
>
> (C + V + E + T)

1. Initial consonant + Vowel

C	+	V		C	+	V	
ก	+	-ะ	กะ gà	ฝ	+	-า	ฝา făa
จ	+	-ิ	จิ jì	ป	+	-ี	ปี pii
ข	+	เ-	เข khěh	ห	+	แ-	แห hăeh
ด	+	-ุ	ดุ dù	ฟ	+	-ู	ฟู fuu
ง	+	เ-าะ	เงาะ ngàw	บ	+	เ-า	เบา bao
น	+	เ-อะ	เนอะ nér	ธ	+	เ-อ	เธอ therr
ส	+	เ-ีย	เสีย sĭa	ร	+	เ-ือ	เรือ rueah

Practice 1: Combine consonants and vowels to form syllables. The first one has been done as an example.

C+V	ต + เ_า	ช + -อ	ผ + เ-อ	ย + ำ	ท + ื	ว + แ-ะ
Syllable	เตา					

C+V	พ + ุ	ส + ใ-	ม + ือ	ต + โ-	ฮ + เ_ย	บ + ๊ว
Syllable						

2. Initial consonant + Vowel + Ending

C	V	E	Syllable
จ	-า	ก	= จาก jàak
พ	ู	ด	= พูด phûut
ร	ี	บ	= รีบ rîip
ข	แ-	น	= แขน khǎehn
ป	โ-	ง	= โปง pohng

Practice 2: Combine consonants, vowels, and endings to form syllables. The first one has been done as an example.

C+V+E	บ + เ- + น	ส + -อ + บ	ป + เ_ย + ก	ย + ุ + ง
Syllable	เบน			

C+V+E	ค + ี + น	ผ + แ- + ด	ด + เือ + ย	จ + ี + น
Syllable				

3. Initial consonant + Vowel + Ending (optional) + Tone mark

C	V	E	T	Syllable
ฝ	-ุ	น	I	= ฝุ่น fùn
ร	-า	น	๋	= ร้าน ráan
จ	เ◌ื◌	ด	๊	= จื๊ด jíit
ต	◌ัว	-	✚	= ตั๋ว tǔa

Practice 3: Combine consonants, vowels, endings and tone marks to form syllables. The first one has been done as an example.

C+V+E+T	พ + เ◌ื◌ + น + ̀	ช + -อ + น + ๋	ต + ◌ือ + ๊
Syllable	เพื่อน		

C+V+E+T	ด + -ุ + ✚	ม + ไ- + ̀	ป + เ◌ะ + ๊
Syllable			

Practice reading and writing the following vocabulary.

1. Pronoun

ฉัน **chăn** I / me (female)	
ผม **phŏm** I / me (male)	
คุณ **khun** you	
เขา **khăo** he / she	
เรา **rao** we	

2. Food & Cooking

หมู mǒu pork	
ไก่ gài chicken	
ปลา plaa fish	
กุ้ง gûng shrimp, prawn	
ไข่ khài egg	
ข้าว khâaw rice	
ข้าวเหนียว khâaw nǐaw sticky rice	
ผัก phàk vegetable	
น้ำ nám water	
ผลไม้ phǒn-lá-mái fruit	
ทำ อาหาร tham-aa-hǎan cook	
ต้ม tôm boil	
ทอด thâwd deep-fry	
ผัด phàt stir-fry	
ย่าง yâang grill	

นึ่ง nûeng steam	
กิน gin eat	
ชอบ châwp like	
หิว hĭw hungry	
อร่อย à-ràwy delicious	
เผ็ด phèt spicy	
หวาน wǎan sweet	
เค็ม khem salty	
เปรี้ยว prîaw sour	

3. Shopping for clothes

เสื้อ sûea shirt	
กางเกง gaang-geng pants	
กระโปรง grà-prong skirt	
กระเป๋า grà-pào purse, bag	
รองเท้า rawng-tháo shoe	

ถุงเท้า **thŭng- tháo** sock	
ซื้อ **súe** buy	
เล็ก **lék** small	
ใหญ่ **yài** large	
ลอง **lawng** try on	
ลด **lót** discount	

4. Colors

สี **sĭi** color	
ดำ **dam** black	
แดง **daehng** red	
ขาว **khăaw** white	
น้ำเงิน **nám-ngerrn** navy blue	
ฟ้า **fáa** blue	
เหลือง **lŭeang** yellow	
ส้ม **sôm** orange	

เขียว **khǐaw** green	
ชมพู **chom-phuu** pink	
ม่วง **mûang** purple	
น้ำตาล **náam-taan** brown	

5. In a House

ห้อง **hâwng** room	
ห้องนั่งเล่น **hâwng nâng lêhn** living room	
ห้องนอน **hâwng nawn** bedroom	
ห้องครัว **hâwng khrua** kitchen	
ห้องน้ำ **hâwng náam** bathroom	
ห้องทำงาน **hâwng tham-ngaan** study room	
โต๊ะ **tó** table	
เก้าอี้ **gâo-îi** chair	
โคมไฟ **khohm-fai** lamp	
โซฟา **soh-faa** sofa	

ตู้ tûu cabinet	
ตู้เย็น tûu yen refrigerator	
แอร์ aeh air conditioner	
หมอน mǎwn pillow	
เตียง tiang bed	
หน้าต่าง nâa-tàang window	

6. Family Members

ครอบครัว khrâwp-khrua family	
ปู่ pùu paternal grandfather	
ย่า yâa paternal grandmother	
ตา taa maternal grandfather	
ยาย yaay maternal grandmother	
พ่อ phâw father	
แม่ mâeh mother	
พี่ชาย phîi-chaay elder brother	

พี่สาว **phîi-săaw** elder sister	
น้องชาย **náwng-chaay** younger brother	
น้องสาว **náwng-săaw** younger sister	
สามี **săa-mii** husband	
ภรรยา **phan-yaa** wife	
ลูกชาย **lûuk-chaay** son	
ลูกสาว **lûuk- săaw** daughter	

7. Occupations

อาจารย์ **aa-jaan** lecturer	
นักศึกษา **nák-sùek-săa** university student	
นักธุรกิจ **nák-thú-rá-gìt** businessman	
หมอ **măw** doctor	
พยาบาล **phá-yaa-baan** nurse	
ตำรวจ **tam-rùat** police officer	

ทหาร **thá-hăan** soldier	
ชาวนา **chaaw-naa** (rice) farmer	

8. Daily routines

นอน **nawn** sleep	
ตื่น **tùen** wake up/get up	
แปรงฟัน **praehng-fan** brush teeth	
ล้างหน้า **láang-nâa** wash face	
อาบน้ำ **àap-nám** take a shower	
สระผม **sà-phŏm** wash hair	
ล้างจาน **láang-jaan** wash dishes	
ซักผ้า **sák-phâa** wash clothes	
อ่านหนังสือ **àan-nŭng-sŭe** read a book	
ทำงาน **tham-ngaan** work	
ประชุม **prà-chum** have a meeting	

9. Places

ห้าง **hâang** department store	
ร้านกาแฟ **ráan-gaa-faeh** coffee shop	
ร้านหนังสือ **ráan-năng-sŭeh** bookstore	
โรงหนัง **rohng-năng** movie theater	
โรงแรม **rong-raehm** hotel	
โรงพยาบาล **rohng-phá-yaa-baan** hospital	
ธนาคาร **thá-na-khaan** bank	
ไปรษณีย์ **prai-sà-nii** post office	
สถานีตำรวจ **sà-thăa-nii-tam-rùat** police station	
โรงเรียน **rong-rian** school	
มหาวิทยาลัย **má-hăa-wít-thá-yaa-lai** university	
บ้าน **bâan** house/home	
วัด **wát** temple	
พิพิธภัณฑ์ **phí-phít-thá-phan** museum	

ตลาด tà-làat market	
แม่น้ำ mâeh-náam river	
น้ำตก náam-tòk waterfall	
ทะเล thá-leh beach	
ภูเขา phuu-khǎo mountain	

10. Hobbies

วิ่ง wîng run	
ขี่จักรยาน khìi-jàk-gà-yaan ride a bike	
เดินป่า derrn-pàa hike	
ทำสวน tham-sǔan gardening	
เต้น tên dance	
ฟังเพลง fang-phlehn listen to music	
ร้องเพลง ráwng-phlehng sing	
เล่นดนตรี lên-don-trii play musical instruments	
ไปเที่ยว pai-thîaw take a trip, travel	

11. Feelings

หิว hĭw hungry	
หิวน้ำ hĭw-nám thirsty	
อิ่ม im full	
ง่วงนอน ngûang-nawn sleepy	
เบื่อ bùea bored	
สนุก sà-nùk enjoyable/fun	
อาย aay shy	
กลัว glua scared	
โกรธ gròht angry	
เครียด khrîat stressed	
ตื่นเต้น tùen-tên excited	
ดีใจ dii-jai happy	
เสียใจ sĭa-jai sad	
กลุ้มใจ glûm-jai worried	
ตกใจ tòk-jai get frightened	

12. Parts of a Body

หน้า **nâa** face	
ผม **phŏm** hair	
หัว **hŭa** head	
ตา **taa** eye	
หู **hŭu** ear	
คอ **khaw** neck	
จมูก **jà-mùuk** nose	
ปาก **pàak** mouth	
ฟัน **fan** teeth	
ท้อง **thâwng** abdomen	
มือ **mueh** hand	
แขน **khăehn** arm	
ขา **khăa** leg	
เท้า **tháo** foot	

13. Sickness

ไม่สบาย mâi-sà-baay sick/ill	
เจ็บ jèp hurt/sore	
เป็นหวัด pen-wàt common cold	
เป็นไข้ pen-khâi fever	
ปวดหัว pùat-hǔa headache	
ปวดฟัน pùat-fan toothache	
ปวดท้อง pùat-tháwng stomachache	
ปวดหลัง pùat-lǎng backache	
เจ็บตา jèp-taa sore eyes	
เจ็บคอ jèp-khaw sore throat	
ไอ ai cough	
อาเจียน aa-jian vomiting	
ท้องเสีย tháwng-sǐa diarrhea	
เป็นผื่น pen-phùen skin rash	

แผล **phlǎeh** cut/wound	
อาหารเป็นพิษ **aa-hǎan-pen-phít** food poisoning	

14. Modes of Transport

แท็กซี่ **táek-sîi** taxi	
รถไฟ **rót-fai** train	
รถเมล์ **rót-may** metro bus	
รถไฟฟ้า **rót-fai-fáa** skytrain (BTS)	
รถไฟใต้ดิน **rót-fai-tâi-din** subway (MRT)	
รถสองแถว **rót-sǎwng-thǎew** two-row minibus	
รถทัวร์ **rót-thua** coach	
รถเก๋ง **rót-gěng** car	
รถตู้ **rót-tûu** van	
เครื่องบิน **khrûeang-bin** airplane	

15. Appearance and Personality

อ้วน **oûan** fat	
ผอม **phǎwm** skinny	
สูง **sǔung** tall	
เตี้ย **tîa** short (height)	
หล่อ **làw** handsome	
เก่ง **gèng** skillful	
ฉลาด **chà-làat** smart	
ขยัน **khà-yǎn** hardworking	
ขี้เกียจ **khîi-gìat** lazy	
ขี้อาย **khîi-aay** shy	
ร่าเริง **râa-rerrng** cheerful	
ใจดี **jai-dii** kind, nice	
ใจดำ **jai-dam** unkind, mean	
ใจร้อน **jai-ráwn** impatient	
ใจเย็น **jai-yen** calm, patient	

Reading Thai Sentences and Short Paragraphs

The basic sentence structure in Thai is similar to English. You can easily form sentences by following the same word order "Subject-Verb-Object" as in English. There are five basic patterns which most Thai sentences are built. There is no requirement for Subject-Verb agreement in Thai.

Patterns	Sentences	
Subject + Verb (S + V)	ฉัน นอน **chăn nawn**	I sleep.
	น้องสาว ตื่นนอน **náwng-săaw tùehn-nawn**	My sister wakes up.
Subject + Verb + Object (S + V + O)	แม่ของฉัน กิน ไก่ย่าง **mâeh khăwng-chăn gin gài-yâang**	My mom eats grilled chicken.
	ฉัน ไป โรงเรียน **chăn pai rohng-rian**	I go to school.
Subject + Adjective (S + Adj)	ฉัน หิว **chăn hĭw**	I am hungry.
	ไข่ทอด อร่อย **khài-thâwt à-ràwy**	Fried egg is delicious.
Subject + Verb + Adverb (S + V + Adv)	ฉัน อาบน้ำ 7 โมงเช้า **chăn àap-náam jèt mohng-cháo**	I take a bath at 7 am.
	ส้มตำ เผ็ด มาก **sôm-tam phèt mâak**	Som Tom is very spicy.
Subject + Verb *to be* + Noun (S + V. be + N)	พ่อ เป็น นักธุรกิจ **phâw pen nák-thú-rá-gìt**	My dad is a businessman.
	ฉัน อยู่ ประเทศไทย **chăn yùu prà-thêht thai**	I am in Thailand.

Here are some basic rules to help you understand the Thai sentence structure.

- A noun can be a person or thing as well as people. In order to indicate number of things (or people, objects, etc.), you need to add a "classifier." Each object has a specific classifier word that should be used when you are stating the quantity of that object. A simple rule is "**noun + number + classifier.**"

Noun + number + classifier		
ข้าว 4 จาน **khâaw sìi jaan**	rice + four + dishes	= four dishes of rice
น้ำ 3 ขวด **náam sǎam khùat**	water + three + bottles	= three bottles of water

- Thai adjectives can function as the main verb in the sentence without any form of the verb "to be" and are placed after the nouns they are describing as shown in the following examples.

The flower is beautiful	= Flower + beautiful	ดอกไม้สวย **dàwk-mái sǔay**
Thai food is delicious	= Thai food + delicious	อาหารไทย อร่อย **aa-hǎan thai à-ràwy**

- When an adjective combines with a noun, the word order is unlike in English. In Thai they are written in **noun + adjective** as shown in the following examples.

English	Thai	
white house	= house + white	บ้านสีขาว **bâan sǐi-khǎaw**
long hair	= hair + long	ผมยาว **phǒm yaaw**

- In order to form a question, you add a question word at the end of the sentence. Also, no question mark is used to indicate the question in a Thai sentence.

Subject + Verb + Object + <u>Question Word</u>	
คุณทำงานกับใคร **Khun tham-ngaan gàp krai**	<u>Who's</u> working with you?

คุณชื่ออะไร **Khun chûeh à-rai**	<u>What</u> is your name?
ห้องน้ำอยู่ที่ไหน **Hăwng-náam yòu thîi-năi**	<u>Where</u> is the bathroom?
คุณจะกลับบ้านเมื่อไร **Khun jà glàp bâan mûeah-rài**	<u>When</u> will you come home?
คุณร้องไห้ทำไม **Khun ráwng-hâi tham-mai**	<u>Why</u> are you crying?
แม่ของคุณเป็นยังไง **Mâeh khăwng khun pen yang-ngai**	<u>How</u> is your mother?
เสื้อตัวนี้เท่าไร **Sêua tua níi thâo-rài**	<u>How much</u> does this shirt cost?
ครอบครัวของคุณมีกี่คน **Khrâwp-khrua khăwng-khun mii gìi khon**	<u>How many</u> people are there in your family?
คุณพูดภาษาไทยได้ไหม **Khun phûut phaa-săa thai dâi-mái**	<u>Can</u> you speak Thai?
คุณหิวไหม **Khun hĭw mái**	<u>Are</u> you hungry?

Practice reading and writing the following phrase and sentences.

Hello (female speaker)	สวัสดีค่ะ **Sà-wàt-dii khâ**	
Hello (male speaker)	สวัสดีครับ **Sà-wàt-dii khráp**	
I, me	ฉัน (female), ผม (male) **Chăn, Phŏm**	
My name is… .	ฉันชื่อ…/ผมชื่อ… **Chăn chûe / phŏm chûe…**	

I come from… .	ฉัน/ผมมาจากประเทศ …. **Chăn/Phŏm maa jàak prà-thêht à-rai**	
How are you?	สบายดีไหม, เป็นยังไงบ้าง **Sà-baay-dii mái, pen yang-ngai bâang**	
I am fine.	สบายดี **Sà-baay-dii**	
Thank you.	ขอบคุณ **Khàwp-khun**	
Excuse me. / I am sorry.	ขอโทษ **Khăw-thôht**	
That's all right.	ไม่เป็นไร **Mâi-pen-rai**	
I don't understand.	ฉัน/ผมไม่เข้าใจ **Chăn/Phŏm mâi-khâo-jai**	
I don't know.	ฉัน/ผมไม่รู้ **Chăn/Phŏm mâi-rúu**	
Speak slowly, please.	พูดช้าๆ **Phûut cháa-cháa**	
I'm feeling sick	ฉัน/ผมไม่สบาย **Chăn/phŏm mâi sà-baay**	
I am allergic to…	ฉัน/ผมแพ้… **Chăn/phŏm-pháeh…**	
I am tired.	ฉัน/ผมเหนื่อย **Chăn/phŏm nùeahy**	
I am lost.	ฉัน/ผมหลงทาง **Chăn/phŏm lŏng-thaang**	
I am a vegan.	ฉัน/ผมกินเจ **Chăn/phŏm kin jay**	

I am hungry.	ฉัน/ผมหิว **Chăn/phŏm hĭw**	
I am thirsty.	ฉัน/ผมหิวน้ำ **Chăn/phŏm hĭw nám**	
I am already full.	ฉัน/ผมอิ่มแล้ว **Chăn/phŏm ìm láew**	
Where is the bathroom?	ห้องน้ำอยู่ที่ไหน **Hâwng-nám yóu thîi-năi**	
How much is it?	เท่าไร **Thâo-rài**	
Can you lower the price?	ลดได้ไหม **Lót dâi-mái**	
Can I try it on?	ลองได้ไหม **Lawng dâi-mái**	
Can you help me?	ช่วยฉัน/ผมได้ไหม **Chûay chăn/phŏm dâi-mái**	
What time is it?	กี่โมง **Gìi-mohng**	
Can you speak English?	คุณพูดภาษาอังกฤษได้ไหม **Khun phûut phaa-săa-ang-grìt dâi-mái**	
How do you say this in Thai?	ภาษาไทยพูดยังไง **Phaa-săa-thai phûut yang-ngai**	
I can speak a bit of Thai.	ฉัน/ผมพูดภาษาไทยได้นิดหน่อย **Chăn/phŏm phûut phaa-săa thai dâi nít-nàwy**	
Please say that again.	พูดอีกทีได้ไหม **Phûut ìik thii dâi-mái**	
How old are you?	คุณอายุเท่าไร **Khun aa-yú thâo-rài**	

What do you do?	คุณทำงานอะไร **Khun tham-ngaan à-rai**	
I am a university student.	ฉัน/ผมเป็นนักศึกษา **Chăn/phŏm pen nák-sùek-săa**	
What do you like to do (in your free time)?	เวลาว่างคุณชอบทำอะไร **Weh-laa-wâang khun châwp tham à-rai**	
I enjoy swimming.	ฉัน/ผมชอบว่ายน้ำ **Chăn/phŏm châwp wâay nám**	
What's your favorite food?	คุณชอบกินอะไร **Khun châwp gin à-rai**	
I like green curry.	ฉัน/ผมชอบกิน แกงเขียวหวาน **Chăn/phŏm châwp gin gaehng-khĭaw-wăan**	
I cannot eat spicy food.	ฉัน/ผมกินเผ็ดไม่ได้ **Chăn/phŏm gin phèt mâi-dâi**	
Do you have an English menu?	มีเมนูภาษาอังกฤษไหม **Mii meh-nuu phaa-săa-ang-grìt mái**	
Today is Monday.	วันนี้วันจันทร์ **Wan-níi wan-jan**	
I go to work at 8 a.m.	ฉัน/ผมไปทำงาน 8 โมงเช้า **Chăn/phŏm pai tham-ngaan pàeht mohng cháo**	
I go back home at 6 p.m.	ฉัน/ผมกลับบ้าน 6 โมงเย็น **Chăn/phŏm glàp bâan hòk mohng yen**	
Can I have your cellphone number?	ขอเบอร์มือถือได้ไหม **Khăw berr mueh-thŭeh dâi-mái**	

Can I have your address?	ขอที่อยู่ได้ไหม **Khăw thîi-yùu dâi-mái**	
Do you have Facebook?	คุณมีเฟซบุ๊คไหม **Khun mii féht-búk mái**	
Happy New Year!	สวัสดีปีใหม่ **Sà-wàt-dii pii-mài**	
Happy Birthday!	สุขสันต์วันเกิด **Sùk-săn wan-gèrrt**	
Congratulations!	ขอแสดงความยินดี **Khăw sà-daehng khwaam yin-dii**	

Reading 1:

แกงเขียวหวานไก่	หอยทอด	ข้าวผัดสับปะรด	ปลาราดพริก
กุ้งชุบแป้งทอด	พะแนงไก่	หมูทอดกระเทียม	ยำถั่วพลูกุ้ง
ผัดเปรี้ยวหวาน	แกงเหลืองปลา	ต้มยำกุ้ง	ผัดกะเพราหมู
น้ำพริกปลาย่าง	ยำปลาดุกฟู	ลาบไก่	ปีกไก่ทอดน้ำแดง

Find the dishes that have the following words.

1. Fish

_____

2. Chicken

_____

3. Shrimp

_____

4. Deep-fry

_____

5. Stir-fry

_____

🎧 Reading 2:

แม่หากระต่ายมาให้ฉันเลี้ยงหนึ่งคู่ กระต่ายตัวหนึ่งมีสีขาวตาสีแดง
กระต่ายอีกตัวหนึ่งสีเทาตาสีดำ ทุกเช้าฉันถือมีดไปตัดหญ้ามาให้กระต่ายกิน บางวันฉันก็
จะมีข้าวโพดมาให้กระต่ายกิน กระต่ายชอบกินข้าวโพดและหญ้า

Vocabulary

กระต่าย	**grà-tàay**	rabbit
เลี้ยง	**líang**	to raise
ถือ	**thǔeh**	to hold, carry
มีด	**mîit**	knife
ตัด	**tàt**	to cut
หญ้า	**yâa**	grass
ข้าวโพด	**khâaw-phôht**	corn

Questions

1. แม่หากระต่ายมาให้ฉันเลี้ยงกี่ตัว

   ก. 1 ตัว   ข. 2 ตัว   ค. 3 ตัว

2. กระต่ายสีเทามีตาสีอะไร

   ก. สีฟ้า   ข. สีแดง   ค. สีดำ

3. ฉันไปตัดหญ้าตอนไหน

   ก. เช้า   ข. บ่าย   ค. เย็น

4. ฉันใช้อะไรตัดหญ้า

   ก. กรรไกร   ข. ขวาน   ค. มีด

5. กระต่าย<u>ไม่</u>ได้กินอะไร

   ก. หัวผักกาด   ข. ข้าวโพด   ค. ยอดหญ้า

🎧 Reading 3:

"แอนน์" เป็นนักศึกษา เขามาจากประเทศอังกฤษ เขาเรียนภาษาไทยที่
มหาวิทยาลัยขอนแก่น ตอนนี้รู้ภาษาไทยนิดหน่อย เมื่อเขาไม่รู้จักคำภาษาไทย
เขาจะถามอาจารย์ว่า นี่อะไร นั่นอะไร โน่นอะไร อาจารย์จะตอบว่า นี่เรียกว่าดินสอ
นั่นเรียกว่าปากกา โน่นเรียกว่าโต๊ะ ที่มหาวิทยาลัยแอนน์เรียนหนัก เพราะเขาเรียน พูด
ฟัง อ่าน และเขียน ภาษาไทย แต่เขา ยังมีเวลาว่างไปเที่ยวกับเพื่อน แอนน์ชอบเรียนภาษา
ไทยและชอบเมืองไทยมาก

Vocabulary

ห้องเรียน	**hâwng-rian**	classroom
รู้, รู้จัก	**rúu, rúu-jàk**	to know
คำ	**kham**	word
ถาม	**thǎam**	to ask
ตอบ	**tàwp**	to answer
มหาวิทยาลัย	**má-hǎa-wít-thá-yaa-lai**	university
เรียน	**rian**	to learn
หนัก	**nàk**	hard
เวลาว่าง	**weh-laa-wâang**	free time
เพื่อน	**phûeahn**	friend

Questions

1. แอนน์มาจากประเทศอะไร

2. เขาเรียนภาษาไทยที่ไหน

3. เมื่อไม่รู้จักคำไทย แอนน์ถามใคร

4. ที่มหาวิทยาลัยแอนน์เป็นอย่างไรบ้าง

5. เมื่อมีเวลาว่างเขาไปเที่ยวกับใคร

6. เขาชอบเรียนภาษาไทยไหม

🎧 Reading 4:

ทุกวันในตอนเย็นเมื่อ 'ขนุน' กลับจากโรงเรียนจะรีบทำการบ้าน เมื่อทำ
การบ้านเสร็จแล้วขนุนจะช่วยแม่เช็ดใบตองเพื่อทำขนมในตอนเช้า แม่ชมขนุนว่า
"ขนุนเป็นเด็กเรียบร้อย ขยัน ชอบช่วยทำงานบ้านทุกวัน" หลังจากช่วยแม่เช็ดใบตองเสร็จ
แล้ว ขนุนจะนั่งอ่านหนังสือ แม่พูดว่า "ถ้าอ่านหนังสือบ่อย ๆ จะทำให้อ่านเก่งและเขียนภา
ษาไทยได้ถูกต้องด้วย" ขนุนอยากเป็นคนเก่งจึงอ่านหนังสือทุกวัน

Vocabulary

ทำการบ้าน	**tham gaan-bâan**	do homework
เช็ด	**chét**	to wipe
ใบตอง	**bai-tawng**	pandan leaf
เรียบร้อย	**rîap-ráwy**	polite
งานบ้าน	**ngaan bâan**	chore
เสร็จแล้ว	**sèt láehw**	finished
ชม	**chom**	to compliment
รีบ	**rîip**	hurry, rush
อ่านหนังสือ	**àan nǎng-sǔeh**	to read (a book)
บ่อย	**bàwy**	often
ถูกต้อง	**thùuk-tâwng**	correct
เก่ง	**gèhng**	skillful

Questions

1. กลับจากโรงเรียนขนุนทำอะไร

2. ตอนเย็นขนุนจะช่วยแม่ทำอะไร

3. แม่ชมขนุนว่าอย่างไร

4. หลังจากช่วยแม่เสร็จแล้ว ขนุนจะทำอะไร

5. ถ้าอ่านหนังสือบ่อยๆ จะทำให้ขนุนเป็นอย่างไร

🎧 Reading 5:

ฉันมีเพื่อนชื่อป้อง พ่อของเขาเป็นหมอ ส่วนแม่เป็นนางพยาบาล ป้องใฝ่ฝันอยากเป็นนักกีฬามาก เขาวิ่งแข่งชนะเพื่อนอยู่เสมอ จนใครๆเรียกเขาว่านักวิ่งลมกรด เพราะเขาวิ่งเร็วเหมือนลมกรดนั่นเอง ฉันและป้อง อยู่บ้านติดกันและอยู่ใกล้ตลาดซึ่งไม่ไกลจากโรงเรียนนัก ป้องชอบออกกำลังกาย เขา กับฉันเดินไปโรงเรียนด้วยกันทุกวัน เวลากลับจากโรงเรียน เขามักจะแวะที่ตลาดเพื่อ ซื้อผลไม้ไปฝากตาของเขา แม่ค้ารู้จักป้องดีเพราะเป็นลูกค้าประจำจึงแถมผลไม้ ให้ทุกครั้ง แม่ค้าคนนี้ตลกมาก แกล้งทำเป็นคิดราคาผลไม้ไม่ได้ ต้องให้ป้องคิดให้ พอเห็นป้องคิดได้ แม่ค้าก็หยิบผลไม้แถมให้อีก ชมป้องว่าน่ารักและเก่งมาก

Vocabulary

ใฝ่ฝัน	**fài-fǎn**	to hope for
นักกีฬา	**nák-gii-laa**	athlete
แข่ง	**khàehng**	to compete
ชนะ	**chá-ná**	to win
นักวิ่ง	**nák-wîng**	runner
ลมกรด	**lom gròt**	jet streams
เร็ว	**rew**	fast
ติดกัน	**tìt gan**	next to
ด้วยกัน	**dûay gan**	together
แวะ	**wáe**	to stop by
ซื้อ...ไปฝาก	**súeh pai fàak**	to buy something for someone
แม่ค้า	**mâeh-kháa**	female vendor
ลูกค้าประจำ	**lûuk-kháa prà-jam**	loyal customer
แถม	**thǎehm**	to give away for free
ตลก	**tà-lòk**	funny
แกล้ง	**glâehng**	to pretend
คิดราคา	**khít ra-khaa**	to calculate a selling price
น่ารัก	**nâa-rák**	a lovely character

1. แม่ของป้องทำงานอะไร
2. ป้องใฝ่ฝันอยากเป็นอะไร
3. ป้องซื้อผลไม้ที่ไหน
4. ป้องซื้อผลไม้ไปฝากใคร
5. ทำไมใครๆ จึงเรียกป้องว่านักวิ่งลมกรด

🎧 Reading 6: A short tale

     บ้านหลังหนึ่งมีหนูชุกชุมมาก เจ้าของบ้านจึงนำแมวมาเลี้ยงไว้เพื่อกำจัด หนู วันหนึ่งแมวเริ่มเห็นว่ามีหนูอยู่ในบ้านเต็มไปหมด จึงคอยจับหนูกินทีละตัว ๆ ทุกวันจนกระทั่งหนูค่อยๆ ลดจำนวนลง พวกหนูที่เหลือรู้สึกเป็นห่วงความปลอดภัยของตัว เอง จึงตกลงกันว่าจะหาอาหารบริเวณที่ใกล้กับรูเท่านั้นเพื่อที่จะหลบเข้ารูได้ทันเมื่อแมวเข้า มาใกล้ และจะไม่ลงไปกินอาหารที่ห้องครัวอีกเป็นอันขาด

     หลังจากนั้นแมวที่เฝ้าอยู่ตรงห้องครัวก็ไม่เห็นหนูอีกเลย ทำให้แมวเริ่มสงสัยว่าทำไม พวกหนูจึงไม่ออกมาหาอาหารเหมือนเช่นเคย จึงคิดแผนการหลอกล่อให้หนูออกมาและ แกล้งทำเป็นนอนตายเพื่อให้หนูตายใจ แต่มีหนูตัวหนึ่งรู้ทันว่าแมวกำลังแกล้งตาย จึงค่อย ๆ ย่องออกมาจากรูอย่างช้า ๆ แล้วบอกกับแมวว่า "แมวเจ้าเล่ห์ พวกข้ารู้ดีว่ามันเป็นกลลวง ของเจ้า ข้าและเพื่อนๆ ไม่เชื่อในอุบายตื้นๆ ของเจ้าหรอก" พูดจบหนูก็รีบวิ่งกลับเข้ารู ตามเดิม

Vocabulary

ชุกชุม	**chúk chum**	scores of (large numbers)
เจ้าของ	**jâo khǎwng**	owner.
กำจัด	**gam jàt**	to get rid of
สังเกต	**sǎng gèht**	notice
เป็นห่วง	**pen hùang**	to be worried
ความปลอดภัย	**khwaam plàwt phai**	safety
ตกลงกัน	**tòk-long gan**	consensus
อาหาร	**aa hǎan**	food
เฝ้า	**fâo**	to keep an eye on

รู	ruu	hole
ห้องครัว	hǎwng khruaw	kitchen
แกล้งตาย	glâehng taay	playing dead
แผนการ	phǎehn gaan	plan
หลอกล่อ	làwk lâw	to trick
ออกอุบาย	àwk u-baay	fool someone into something
รู้ทัน	rúu than	realize immediately
ย่อง	yâwng	to tiptoe
เจ้าเล่ห์	jâo-lêh	cunning
กลลวง	gon luang	ruse

Questions

1. เจ้าของบ้านทำอะไรเพื่อกำจัดหนู

2. เพื่อความปลอดภัย พวกหนูที่เหลือตกลงกันว่าจะหาอาหารที่ไหน

3. แมวเฝ้าหนูอยู่ที่ไหน

4. แมวมีแผนการอะไรหลอกล่อให้หนูออกมา

5. ก่อนวิ่งกลับวิ่งกลับเข้ารูตามเดิม หนูพูดอะไรกับแมว

Do-It-Yourself

A. Fill in the following charts by writing Thai consonants, vowels and tone marks in each box. Then check your entries on pages 14–15 (consonants), page 32 (vowels) and page 47 (tone marks) and practice saying them out loud.

Consonants

1. Mid tone consonants

gaw										
jaw										
daw										
daw										
taw										
taw										
baw										
paw										
aw										

2. High tone consonants

khǎw										
chǎw										
thǎw										

thăw										
phăw										
phăw										
săw										
săw										
săw										
hăw										

3. Low tone consonants

khàw										
ngàw										
chàw										
chàw										
sàw										
thàw										
thàw										
thàw										

thàw									
phàw									
phàw									
nàw									
nàw									
fàw									
màw									
yàw									
yàw									
ràw									
làw									
làw									
wàw									
hàw									

Vowels

1. Single vowels

a									
i									
ue									
u									
e									
ae									
o									
aw									
er									
aa									
ii									
ueh									
uu									
eh									

aeh										
oh										
aw										
err										
am										
ai										
ai										
ao										

2. Diphthongs

ia									
uea									
ua									
iaa									
ueah									
uaa									

Tone marks

low											
falling											
high											
rising											

B. Identify the **tones** of these words, and put them into the blank as the following order.

มี	เลี้ยง	เก่ง	ชาย	เริ่ม	ฟ้า
น้อง	สี่	ต้อง	พี่	ซื้อ	เที่ยว
เป็น	วัด	ร้อง	โต๊ะ	เลิก	สวย
ขาย	คอย	ค่ะ	ไข่	น้อย	ห่าม
เล่น	เช้า	นาน	นะ	มาก	จิ๋ว

1. Mid tone   =   _____

2. Low tone   =   _____

3. Falling tone   =   _____

4. High tone   =   _____

5. Rising tone   =   _____

Quizzes

A. Fill the blanks with the correct Thai words from the list on pages 109–110.

Greetings and Basic Phrases

1. Hello _____

2. I, me (female) _____

3. I, me (male) _____

4. name _____

5. My name is… . _____

7. How are you? _____

8. I am fine. _____

9. Thank you. _____

10. Excuse me. / I am sorry. _____

11. You're welcome./ That's all right. _____

12. Speak slowly, please. _____

Countries

1. the United States _____

2. France _____

3. Germany _____

4. Italy _____

5. Russia _____

7. Spain _____

8. Thailand _____

9. India _____

10. China _____

11. Japan _____

12. Korea _____

Cities

1. Bangkok _____

2. Ayutthaya _____

3. Sukhothai _____

4. Kanchanaburi _____

5. Chiang Mai _____

7. Chiang Rai _____

8. Mae Hong Son _____

9. Hua-Hin _____

10. Pattaya _____

11. Phuket _____

12. Krabi _____

อินเดีย	กระบี่	เยอรมัน
สุโขทัย	ฝรั่งเศส	อยุธยา
ผม	กรุงเทพมหานคร	ฉัน
ชื่อ	อิตาลี	สบายดีไหม
ญี่ปุ่น	ขอโทษ	เชียงใหม่
กาญจนบุรี	สเปน	เกาหลี
ภูเก็ต	ไทย	แม่ฮ่องสอน

ขอบคุณ	สวัสดี	หัวหิน
รัสเซีย	จีน	พัทยา
ไม่เป็นไร	ฉัน/ผม ชื่อ	พูดช้า ๆ
สบายดี	เชียงราย	อเมริกา

B. Fill in the blanks with appropriate Romanization.

Food

1. หมู   _____   pork

2. ไก่   _____   chicken

3. ปลา   _____   fish

4. กุ้ง   _____   shrimp, prawn

5. ไข่   _____   egg

7. ข้าว   _____   rice

8. ข้าวเหนียว   _____   sticky rice

9. ข้าวผัด   _____   fried rice

10. ผัก   _____   vegetable

11. น้ำ   _____   water

12. ผลไม้   _____   fruit

13. ไข่ดาว   _____   fried egg

14. แกงเขียวหวานไก่   _____   green curry with chicken

15. ต้มยำกุ้ง   _____   prawn and lemongrass soup

16. ผัดไทย   _____   Thai fried noodle

17. ผัดผัก   _____   stir-fried vegetable

18. ส้มตำ	_____	papaya salad
19. ไก่ย่าง	_____	grilled chicken
20. ก๋วยเตี๋ยว	_____	noodle
21. ขนมปัง	_____	bread
22. ชีส	_____	cheese
23. เนย	_____	butter
24. แฮมเบอร์เกอร์	_____	hamburger
25. สเต็ก	_____	steak
26. เฟรนช์ฟรายส์	_____	French fries
27. สลัด	_____	salad
28. สปาเก็ตตี้	_____	spaghetti
29. ไอศครีม	_____	ice cream
30. เค้ก	_____	cake
31. น้ำผลไม้	_____	juice
32. เบียร์	_____	beer
33. ไวน์	_____	wine
34. กาแฟ	_____	coffee
35. ชามะนาว	_____	lemon tea
36. ชาเขียว	_____	green tea
38. ส้ม	_____	orange
39. กล้วย	_____	banana
40. สับปะรด	_____	pineapple

41. แตงโม _____ watermelon

42. แอปเปิล _____ apple

43. พริก _____ chili pepper

44. เกลือ _____ salt

45. น้ำตาล _____ sugar

46. น้ำปลา _____ fish sauce

47. เผ็ด _____ spicy

48. หวาน _____ sweet

49. เค็ม _____ salty

50. เปรี้ยว _____ sour

Places

1. ร้านกาแฟ _____ coffee shop

2. ร้านหนังสือ _____ bookstore

3. โรงหนัง _____ movie theater

4. โรงแรม _____ hotel

5. โรงพยาบาล _____ hospital

7. ธนาคาร _____ bank

8. ไปรษณีย์ _____ post office

9. สถานีตำรวจ _____ police station

10. วัด _____ temple

11. พิพิธภัณฑ์ _____ museum

12. โรงเรียน _____ school

13. มหาวิทยาลัย _____ university

14. แม่น้ำ _____ river

15. น้ำตก _____ waterfall

16. ภูเขา _____ mountain

17. ทะเล _____ beach/ocean

Family members

1. ครอบครัว _____ family

2. ปู่ _____ paternal grandfather

3. ย่า _____ paternal grandmother

4. ตา _____ maternal grandfather

5. ยาย _____ maternal grandmother

7. พ่อ _____ father

8. แม่ _____ mother

9. พี่ชาย _____ elder brother

10. พี่สาว _____ elder sister

11. น้องชาย _____ younger brother

12. น้องสาว _____ younger sister

13. ลุง _____ uncle

14. ป้า _____ older sister of one's father or mother

15. น้า/อา _____ younger sister/brother of one's father or mother

16. สามี _____ husband

17. ภรรยา   _____   wife

18. ลูกสาว   _____   daughter

19. ลูกชาย   _____   son

20. พี่น้อง   _____   siblings

C. Find words from the list on page 115 and put them in the correct category. Then write the English translation of each word next to it. You can use a dictionary if necessary.

Work and Play

Occupations		Hobbies	
Thai	English	Thai	English

ชาวนา	ทำสวน	ร้องเพลง	อาจารย์
ฟังเพลง	นักการเมือง	ทหาร	เต้น
หมอ	พยาบาล	ว่ายน้ำ	ทนาย
เดินป่า	เล่นดนตรี	ขี่จักรยาน	ดูหนัง
นักศึกษา	วิ่ง	นักธุรกิจ	ตำรวจ

Writing a Paragraph

About Thailand

Copy each line in the space provided.

ประเทศไทยอยู่ในภูมิภาคเอเชียตะวันออกเฉียงใต้ ติดกับทะเลอันดามันและอ่าวไทย

_____

_____

ด้านทิศตะวันออกติดกับ ประเทศลาวและกัมพูชาด้านทิศเหนือและทิศตะวันตกติดกับประ
เทศพม่า และทิศใต้ติดกับประเทศมาเลเซีย

_____

_____

ประเทศไทยมี 77 จังหวัด แบ่งออกเป็น 4 ภาค คือ ภาคเหนือ ภาคตะวันออกเฉียงเหนือ
ภาคกลาง และ ภาคใต้ เมืองหลวงคือกรุงเทพมหานคร

_____

_____

ประเทศไทยมี 3 ฤดูคือ ฤดูร้อน ฤดูฝน ฤดูหนาว

_____

_____

เดือนเมษายนและพฤษภาคมเป็นเดือนที่ร้อนที่สุดของปี ฤดูฝนเริ่มจากมิถุนายนจนถึงปลาย
เดือนตุลาคม และ ฤดูหนาวตั้งแต่เดือนพฤศจิกายนถึงกุมภาพันธ์

_____

_____

ประเทศไทยมีสถานที่ท่องเที่ยวหลากหลาย เช่น ภูเขา น้ำตก ทะเล อุทยานแห่งชาติ
และเกาะต่างๆ

_____

_____

อาหารไทยที่มีชื่อเสียงคือ ผัดไทยกับต้มยำกุ้ง

_____

_____

Self-introduction

Use this self-introduction as a model to write about yourself in Thai.

My name is Jane. I live in Sydney, Australia. I am 19 years old. There are five people in my family. My father is a police officer, and my mother is a nurse. I have an elder brother and one younger sister. My brother, Jack, works as a lawyer. My younger sister, Julie, is a high school student. I'm studying Thai at university. In my free time, I like watching movies and listening to music.

ฉันชื่อเจน ฉันอยู่เมืองซิดนีย์ ประเทศออสเตรเลีย ฉันอายุ 19 ปี ครอบครัวของฉันมี 5 คน พ่อของฉันเป็นตำรวจและแม่ของฉันเป็นพยาบาล ฉันมีพี่ชายกับน้องสาว พี่ชายของฉันชื่อแจ๊คเป็นทนาย น้องสาวของฉันชื่อจูลี่เป็นนักเรียน ฉันเรียนภาษาไทยที่มหาวิทยาลัย เวลาว่างฉันชอบดูหนังกับฟังเพลง

_____

_____

_____

_____

About your travel memory

Use this writing as a model to write about your trip in Thai.

I went to Thailand last year. It was fun. I was in Bangkok for three days. I went shopping at Chatuchak Weekend Market, and took the boat tours to explore the surrounding canals and rivers. Houses and restaurants are along the rivers as in Venice. There are several floating markets in Bangkok and I went to one of them called Taling Chan Floating Market. There was music, food, arts and loads of fruits. The food in Bangkok was delicious and I ate a lot of mangoes.

_____

_____

_____

_____

Part

3

Appendices

Appendix 1: Thai Basic Phrases

How are you?	สบายดีไหม, เป็นยังไงบ้าง	sà-baay-dii mái, pen yang-ngai bâang
I am fine.	สบายดี	sà-baay-dii
Thank you.	ขอบคุณ	khàwp-khun
Excuse me. / I am sorry.	ขอโทษ	khǎw-thôht
That's all right.	ไม่เป็นไร	mâi-pen-rai
I don't understand.	ฉัน/ผม ไม่เข้าใจ	chǎn/phǒm mâi-khâo-jai
I don't know.	ฉัน/ผม ไม่รู้	chǎn/phǒm mâi-rúu
Speak slowly, please.	พูดช้าๆ	phûut cháa-cháa
I'd like... (for request)	ขอ...	khǎw...
I am hungry.	ฉัน/ผม หิว	chǎn/phǒm hǐw
I am thirsty.	ฉัน/ผม หิวน้ำ	chǎn/phǒm hǐw nám
I am already full.	ฉัน/ผม อิ่มแล้ว	chǎn/phǒm ìm láew
Where is the bathroom?	ห้องน้ำอยู่ที่ไหน	hâwng-nám yóu thîi-nǎi?
Can you lower the price?	ลดได้ไหม	lót dâi-mái
Can you help me?	ช่วย ฉัน/ผม ได้ไหม	chûay chǎn/phǒm dâi-mái
Can you speak English?	คุณพูดภาษาอังกฤษได้ไหม	khun phûut phaa-sǎa-ang-grìt dâi-mái
What is this?	นี่อะไร	nîi à-rai
How do you say this in Thai?	ภาษาไทยพูดยังไง	phaa-sǎa-thai phûut yang-ngai
I'm feeling sick.	ฉัน/ผม ไม่สบาย	chǎn/phǒm mâi sà-baay
I am lost.	ฉัน/ผม หลงทาง	chǎn/phǒm lǒng-thaang

Appendix 2: Classifiers

cube (ice, sugar)	ก้อน	**gâwn**
branch of tree	กิ่ง	**gìng**
bottle	ขวด	**khùat**
people	คน	**khon**
car, motorcycle, bicycle	คัน	**khan**
pair of ...	คู่	**khûu**
piece of ...	ชิ้น	**chín**
animal, table, chair, clothing	ตัว	**tua**
container, leaf, baggage	ใบ	**bai**
blanket, towel, piece of cloth	ผืน	**phǔehn**
sheet of paper	แผ่น	**phàehn**
fruit, mountain	ลูก	**lûuk**
boat, airplane	ลำ	**lam**
book, notebook, knife	เล่ม	**lêhm**
house, building	หลัง	**lǎng**
flower, key	ดอก	**dàwk**
piece of ...	อัน	**an**

Appendix 3: Vegetables

Sweet basil	กะเพรา	**gà-phrao**
Cabbage	กะหล่ำปลี	**gà-làm-plii**
Cauliflower	กะหล่ำดอก	**gà-làm-dàwk**
Turmeric	ขมิ้น	**khà-mîn**
Galangal	ข่า	**khàa**
Corn	ข้าวโพด	**khâaw-phôht**
Ginger	ขิง	**khǐng**
Lemonglass	ตะไคร้	**tà-khrái**
Cucumber	แตงกวา	**taehng-gwaa**
Yardlong bean	ถั่วฝักยาว	**thùa-fàk-yaaw**
Groundnut	ถั่วลิสง	**thùa-lí-sǒng**
Soybean	ถั่วเหลือง	**thùa-lǔeahng**
Chinese radish	ผักกาดหัว, หัวไชเท้า	**phàk-gàat-hǔa, hǔa-chai-tháo**
Chinese cabbage	ผักกวางตุ้ง	**phàk-gwaang-tûng**
Lettuce	ผักกาด	**phàk-gàat**
Kale	ผักคะน้า	**phàk-khá-náa**
Morning glory	ผักบุ้ง	**phàk-bûng**
Taro	เผือก	**phùeahk**
Chili	พริก	**phrík**
Pepper	พริกไทย	**phrík-thai**
Pumpkin	ฟักทอง	**fák-thawng**

Leech lime	มะกรูด	má-grùut
Tomato	มะเขือเทศ	má-khǔeah-thêht
Onion	หอมหัวใหญ่	hǎwm-hǔa-yài
Pickle	ผักดอง	phàk-dawng
Bamboo shoot	หน่อไม้	nàw-mái
Carrot	แครอท	khaeh-ràwt

Appendix 4: Fruits

Durian	ทุเรียน	thú-rian
Rambutan	เงาะ	ngáw
Mangosteen	มังคุด	mang-khút
Mango	มะม่วง	má-mûang
Papaya	มะละกอ	má-lá-gaw
Pineapple	สับปะรด	sàp-pà-rót
Jackfruit	ขนุน	khà-nŭn
Lychee	ลิ้นจี่	lín-jìi
Longan	ลำไย	lam-yai
Orange	ส้ม	sôm
Pomelo	ส้มโอ	sôm-oh
Banana	กล้วย	glûay
Watermelon	แตงโม	taehng-moh
Rose apple	ชมพู่	chom-phûu
Guava	ฝรั่ง	fà-ràng
Grape	องุ่น	à-ngùn
Apple	แอปเปิ้ล	áep-pêrn

Appendix 5: Days and Months

Day	วัน	
Monday	วันจันทร์	**wan-jan**
Tuesday	วันอังคาร	**wan-ang-khaan**
Wednesday	วันพุธ	**wan-phút**
Thursday	วันพฤหัสบดี, วันพฤหัส	**wan-phá-rúe-hàt-sà-baw-dii, wan-phá-rúe-hàt**
Friday	วันศุกร์	**wan-sùk**
Saturday	วันเสาร์	**wan-săo**
Sunday	วันอาทิตย์	**wan-aa-thít**

Month	เดือน	
January	มกราคม	**má-gà-raa-khom**
February	กุมภาพันธ์	**gum-phaa-phan**
March	มีนาคม	**mii-naa-khom**
April	เมษายน	**meh-săa-yon**
May	พฤษภาคม	**phrúet-sà-phaa-khom**
Jun	มิถุนายน	**mí-thù-naa-yon**
July	กรกฎาคม	**gà-rá-gà-daa-khom**
August	สิงหาคม	**sĭng-hăa-khom**
September	กันยายน	**gan-yaa-yon**
October	ตุลาคม	**tù-laa-khom**
November	พฤศจิกายน	**phrúet-sà-jì-gaa-yon**
December	ธันวาคม	**than-waa-khom**

Appendix 6: Transport

Car	รถยนต์	rót-yon
Motorcycle	รถมอเตอร์ไซด์	rót-maw-terr-sai
Bike	รถจักรยาน	rót-jàk-grà-yaan
Metro bus	รถเมล์	rót-meh
Coach (bus)	รถบัส, รถทัวร์	rót-bát, rót-thua
Train	รถไฟ	rót-fai
Truck	รถบรรทุก	rót-ban-thúk
Pick-up truck	รถกระบะ	rót-grà-bà
Tricycle	รถสามล้อ	rót-săam-láw
Tuk tuk	รถตุ๊กตุ๊ก	rót-túk-túk
Airplane	เครื่องบิน	khrûeahng-bin
Boat, ship	เรือ	rueah
Sky train	รถไฟฟ้า	rót-fai-fáa
Subway/Underground	รถไฟใต้ดิน	rót-fai tâi-din

Appendix 7: Weight and Length

Millimeter (mm)	มิลลิเมตร	min-lí-méht
Centimeter (cm)	เซนติเมตร	sen-tì-méht
Meter (m)	เมตร	méht
Kilometer (km)	กิโลเมตร	gì-loh-méht
Milligram (mg)	มิลลิกรัม	min-lí-gram
Gram (g)	กรัม	gram
Kilogram (kg)	กิโลกรัม	gì-loh-gram
Milliliter (ml)	มิลลิลิตร	min-lí-lít
Liter (l)	ลิตร	lít
Mile	ไมล์	mai
Inch	นิ้ว	níw
Feet	ฟุต	fút

"Books to Span the East and West"

Tuttle Publishing was founded in 1832 in the small New England town of Rutland, Vermont [USA]. Our core values remain as strong today as they were then—to publish best-in-class books which bring people together one page at a time. In 1948, we established a publishing outpost in Japan—and Tuttle is now a leader in publishing English-language books about the arts, languages and cultures of Asia. The world has become a much smaller place today and Asia's economic and cultural influence has grown. Yet the need for meaningful dialogue and information about this diverse region has never been greater. Over the past seven decades, Tuttle has published thousands of books on subjects ranging from martial arts and paper crafts to language learning and literature—and our talented authors, illustrators, designers and photographers have won many prestigious awards. We welcome you to explore the wealth of information available on Asia at **www.tuttlepublishing.com**.

Published by Tuttle Publishing, an imprint of Periplus Editions (HK) Ltd.

www.tuttlepublishing.com

Copyright © 2022 by Periplus Editions (HK) Ltd.

Photo credits:
Cover image © Shutterstock | Dragon Images, Interiors: p 4 © Shutterstock | Anck.soowannaphoom; p 118 © Shutterstock | Aunging

Library of Congress Control Number: 2022935071

ISBN 978-0-8048-5379-8

Distributed by

North America, Latin America & Europe
Tuttle Publishing
364 Innovation Drive
North Clarendon,
VT 05759-9436 U.S.A.
Tel: 1 (802) 773-8930; Fax: 1 (802) 773-6993
info@tuttlepublishing.com
www.tuttlepublishing.com

Asia Pacific
Berkeley Books Pte. Ltd.
3 Kallang Sector #04-01
Singapore 349278
Tel: (65) 6741-2178; Fax: (65) 6741-2179
inquiries@periplus.com.sg
www.tuttlepublishing.com

26 25 24 23   5 4 3 2
Printed in Singapore   2307MP

TUTTLE PUBLISHING® is a registered trademark of Tuttle Publishing, a division of Periplus Editions (HK) Ltd.